D0343453

"A terrific resource for leadership coaching."

—**Tom Bugielski,** SVP and COO, Republic Bank

"There is a difference between coaching and managing sales professionals. If you don't understand the distinction, you are not getting the most out of your sales team. This new book by Sandler is a great guide to learning to coach and be coached. It speaks of the 'commitment' required to be a good coach. The book is filled with great stories, anecdotes, and what they call 'Sandler Coaching Rules.' It is a great read that is easy to understand and implement ... but you need commitment to succeed."

—**Michael Nick,** author, *Adapt or Fail*

"What is sales coaching? Why is it important? How should coaching for a top sales performer differ from coaching for a mid-level performer or a low-level performer? What does a good coaching session look and sound like? Most sales managers think they know the answers to these questions, but really don't. *The Sales Coach's Playbook* from Sandler Training offers the answers. Indispensable."

—**Karl H. Watson,** President, CEMEX USA

"Sandler's advice on how to more effectively motivate and reinforce salespeople is well worth listening to."

—**Sean Chisholm,** VP of Operations and Strategy, Classy

"Sandler has taken its success in developing great salespeople and created a playbook to help managers have impact through coaching."

—**JOHN A. VACCARO,** Senior Vice President, USIG Sales & Distribution

"*The Sales Coach's Playbook* provided me with immeasurable insights on how to grow, both personally and professionally."

—**JULIE ROGERS,** VP and General Manager, Hireology

"Smart, inspiring, and genuine."

—**DANETTE SWANK,** President, Philippi-Hagenbuch, Inc.

THE
SALES
COACH'S
PLAYBOOK

THE
SALES
COACH'S
PLAYBOOK

Breaking the Performance Code

BILL BARTLETT

Foreword by DAVID MATTSON

Sandler Training

© 2016 Sandler Systems, Inc. All rights reserved.

Reproduction, modification, storage in a retrieval system or re-transmission, in any form or by any means, electronic, mechanical or otherwise, is strictly prohibited without the prior written permission of Sandler Systems, Inc.

S Sandler Training (with design), Sandler, Sandler Training, Sandler Selling System, Sandler Submarine (words and design), and Sandler Pain Funnel are registered service marks of Sandler Systems, Inc.

"The Devine Inventory" is a service mark of The Devine Group, Inc. Used with permission.

"Extended DISC" is a registered trademark of Extended DISC International Oy Ltd. Used with permission.

Because the English language lacks a generic singular pronoun that indicates both genders, we have used the masculine pronouns for the sake of style, readability, and brevity. This material applies to both men and women.

Paperback: 978-0-692-60668-1

E-book: 978-0-692-60672-8

Dedication

To David H. Sandler, who on October 24, 1994, had a profound impact on my life when he allowed me to be a part of his fantastic business community. David's marvelous selling methodology had a deep impact on my professional and personal life.

To David Mattson, whose masterful leadership has taken Sandler Training to a new level of success. He has "raised the river" and with it allowed all boats to rise accordingly.

Acknowledgments

I would like to thank the following individuals for their help and guidance during the writing of this book, all of whom made the journey easier. To my fellow Sandler trainers, you have taught me more than you will ever know. To David Mattson, your strategic insight was invaluable; it created a framework for success. To Yusuf Toropov, your writing experience was a guiding light on the journey. To Laura Matthews and Jerry Dorris, your editing and layout contributions, respectively, were top-notch. To my clients, thanks for placing your trust in coaching and for your commitment to take action on our coaching sessions. To the members of Corporate Strategies & Solutions, Inc, your support for this book project energized me along the way. Last, but certainly not least, my deepest gratitude goes out to Gayle Bartlett; you were an inspiration and you guided me to the finish line. Thank you for your love and support.

CONTENTS

Foreword

As a manager, you always want to make sure that your salespeople are fulfilling their potential. Every single touch point you have with them should be driven by a very simple question: How can you best support them in increasing both their effectiveness (their ability to do the right things) and their efficiency (their ability to do those things well)?

You also have to ask yourself another important question: How do you protect your own precious time? How do you avoid falling into a time trap, day after day? How do you keep yourself out of the stressful scenario in which you solve everyone else's problems—often the same problems over and over again—while your team underperforms?

This book helps you address both big questions. It does that by supporting you in your development as a sales manager within the area that is, potentially, the single highest-impact element of your job: sales coaching.

Many sales leaders underestimate the importance of sales coaching. This happens, at least in part, because they haven't been exposed to the kinds of dramatic performance changes that effective sales coaching can bring about. What's more, they may begin with an incomplete understanding of what effective sales coaching really is. Another challenge is the common preconception that the most important group for the organization to train is the sales team. In most situations, it's just as important that the managers train to improve their skill sets—specifically, the coaching skill set.

In the vast majority of cases, sales managers simply aren't trained to the same level of proficiency demanded of most other job functions within the organization. The accountants and the engineers and the marketing people who work for a given enterprise are all likely to have advanced degrees in their field of specialty, and many of them are busy getting continuing education credits. That's part of their career path. That's expected. Compare that to the situation of the sales manager. Most of the people who wind up in this job didn't get there because they were good managers; they got there because they were good salespeople. They take their new position without any sales management process to follow, and no one shares any process with them. All too often, their professional development plan is ineffective or nonexistent. That's unfortunate for both the individual and the organization because it means that most sales managers do their learning through trial and error.

There are two big problems with trial and error. It's the most expensive training for sales managers out there. And it's slow. While the time passes, teams underperform. Performance goals are missed. People get frustrated. Promising careers are compromised.

As an alternative, this book offers you:

- An overview of the four different jobs a sales manager must be able to do: mentor, trainer, supervisor, and coach. Most sales managers neglect their own development in at least one of those areas.

- An in-depth examination of what is and isn't part of the coaching function. This is essential because often coaching is poorly understood. Managers frequently think they're coaching salespeople, when in fact they're not.

- A proven seven-step methodology for coaching salespeople effectively, based on the principles developed by David H. Sandler, the founder of Sandler Training.

Improving this one area of sales management—coaching—can have a huge positive impact in both the short term and the long term. When properly executed, sales coaching delivers a positive ripple effect that leads to truly remarkable performance turnarounds for both individuals and teams. (By the way, each chapter of this book features a true story of such a turnaround; the names and some identifying details have been altered.)

The program laid out in this book has been proven to work across virtually all industries. It can work for you. It does require an investment of time and attention, and it may challenge you to change some of your existing patterns of behavior. But I would ask you to consider the upside of investing the modest amount of time and personal focus necessary to learn about and master the Sandler Coaching System. Once you master it, you and your organization can fast-forward over years, or even decades, of trial and error.

Whether you are just starting out in the job of sales manager, have been doing the job for a few years, or have been doing it for decades, you will find, in these pages, insights and processes that will accelerate your own learning curve as a manager, extend the productive life cycle of your best performers, and help your team as a whole to achieve at a measurably higher level.

David H. Mattson
President/CEO, Sandler Training

CHAPTER ONE

The Basics

OVERVIEW

- Defining sales coaching
- Why invest time in coaching
- The relationship between coaching and performance
- The big picture of coaching
- Why managers fail at coaching and how to prevent this

I n this chapter, you will learn the importance of coaching and why sales managers must use it to help salespeople grow. There is a direct link between effective coaching and performance improvement; the key to improvement is behavioral modification.

WHAT IS EFFECTIVE SALES COACHING?

There is no one-size-fits-all sales coaching model. There are only approaches that have been shown to be successful in particular situations. The best idea is to identify each individual salesperson's personal "success code"—and use that code to unlock the salesperson's potential for success.

It is up to the coach to choose the right approach for the salesperson and the situation. Effective sales coaching adjusts to particular people and circumstances.

The chapters that follow offer an overview of the sales coaching practices I have found to be most effective over the past four decades, along with a discussion of the situations in which they are most likely to be useful. The "playbook" for effective sales coaching that you are now reading is based on the proven principles of the Sandler Selling System® methodology. It's intended for sales leaders who want to improve their performance within the special role we call "coach"—a role that is, as you will see, distinct

SANDLER COACHING INSIGHT

In order for your sales coaching to be truly effective, first determine the individual salesperson's current level of skill in a given area. Be willing and able to coach to that level of skill, not to a future or desired level of skill. When coaching efforts are unsuccessful, it's usually because the coach has, for one reason or another, overlooked this principle.

from the other three sales management roles of supervisor, mentor, and trainer. If you are such a leader, please do keep reading. You are the person for whom the Sandler® Coaching System was created. Whenever you see the words "coach" and "coaching," please assume I'm talking to and about you.

> **?** **WHAT DOES IT MEAN?**
>
> **Sales coaching** is a formal process that uses one-on-one meetings to help salespeople achieve new levels of success by discovering hidden issues that inhibit their performance. Contrary to popular belief and practice, effective sales coaching is not "showing them how to do it."

CRITICAL BEHAVIOR MODIFICATION

Coaching salespeople for improved performance must begin with a clear understanding of: the individual salesperson's current level of skill; the salesperson's knowledge of the behaviors critical to success in certain selling situations; and the salesperson's self-awareness during the sales process.

In order for your sales coaching to be effective, you must focus on critical behavior modification—not on the imparting of new skills.

The salesperson's current level of effectiveness is always the starting point, along with being the benchmark for improvement over time.

BARB'S STORY

My coaching client Barbara started her business about ten years ago. Barb is a brilliant "idea" person. Her business took off instantly. As she herself said, she "caught lightning in a bottle" and quickly built a customer base. As so often happens, the founder of a young company emerged as its first and best salesperson.

Barb hired a sales team. The company cruised along fine at the beginning, showing consistent growth over its first three years. The idea behind the business was so strong that the business model alone propelled most of the growth during this early phase. In the fourth year, however, the business slowed and eventually stalled.

Barb pushed her salespeople harder than ever before. You see, she knew how great the business could be once again if only her salespeople would do what she, Barbara, would do in various selling situations. She "coached" them by telling them over and over again what to do.

By Year Five, some of Barb's best salespeople had quit because the pressure to perform was too great. The company's downward spiral continued in the first quarter, which was when Barbara reached out to me for help.

We began with a one-on-one coaching process. I met with her weekly. I was eager to learn what was really behind the flattening of her business's revenue streams.

Barb was reluctant, at first, to be vulnerable during our sessions. She blamed her salespeople. It took a few weeks of discussion for us to reach a point where she understood that her salespeople were not the enemy and that she herself played a major role in the problems her business was facing.

In time, we developed a new leadership model, one with which Barb was comfortable. It emphasized coaching, mentoring, and training, de-emphasized the supervisory role (which Barb assigned to someone else), and fit well with her personal management style. This new approach to sales management helped her encourage her salespeople to make and sustain important behavioral changes over time, rather than asking them to master, on the spot, the sales tactics with which Barb herself was most comfortable.

Barb soon gained a much deeper understanding of the issues of each member of the sales team, and she stopped micromanaging. This new style worked well for the remainder of Year Six as well as all of Year Seven. The revenue trend improved. Eventually Barb decided to devote more of her time to running the company; she hired a sales manager with the specific skills necessary to work with the sales force. Barb and I still meet, but now we focus on more strategic issues. My coaching focuses on planning, communication, and the image of Barb's business. This four-year relationship has transformed Barbara as well as her business and has put her on track to achieve the success she deserves.

LANGUAGE MATTERS

The language of an effective coaching session is vitally important, and understanding it is your first responsibility. This language is expressed both verbally and nonverbally.

The most effective coaches understand the nature of nonverbal messaging. They are good at reading body language and tonality to determine a given salesperson's level of buy-in to the coaching process.

Managers must understand that they cannot "sell" coaching to salespeople who don't yet associate it with success. Nothing good results from a coaching session where the salesperson sits quietly and gets involved on an intellectual level but has no emotional ownership of the process. Coaching is most effective when salespeople are willing to be vulnerable and share meaningful experiences. Once they realize that certain behaviors, if changed, will help them improve and create even greater success, they become equal partners in the coaching process. Not before!

Language—spoken and otherwise—is always the gateway to that partnership. The most powerful coaching moments, for salespeople and everyone else, involve individuals analyzing their own deeply held personal beliefs and considering whether those beliefs are driving them toward greater success—or holding them hostage. Far too many salespeople are prisoners of negative patterns resulting from broken personal belief systems that limit their ability to grow. The best coaches know that the language employed during the coaching session is a vitally important tool for creating breakthroughs around the assessment of those belief systems. Accordingly, they choose their words—and their nonverbal messaging—with great care.

Throughout this book, you'll be getting suggestions on how

to interact with salespeople. As you move from thinking about this advice toward putting it into practice, I'd like to ask you to remember this: The words you choose to speak during coaching sessions are important, but they are not the only communication the salesperson with whom you are working will process. The tone of voice you use, the facial expressions you employ, and the way you present yourself physically will also have a powerful impact. Truth be told, these nonverbal messages are more important to the success of your coaching than the words you choose to say. Ultimately, you are responsible for all of the messages you send to the salesperson you are coaching—not just for the recitation of the "right words" during the session.

FOUR THINGS SALES MANAGERS DO

Coaching is one of the most critical elements of leadership of the sales team—or indeed of any team. Coaching supports the other three major functions of leadership: supervising, mentoring, and training.

SANDLER COACHING INSIGHT

Coaching represents about 35% of the successful leadership role and has the single greatest impact on the future success of the salesperson.

Coaching has absolutely nothing to do with directing the actions of the salesperson. It is singularly focused on helping salespeople generate a personal understanding of better ways to act while they are in the selling environment. The successful coach thoroughly understands the seven-step Sandler Selling System and uses that knowledge to help salespeople commit to better execution and improved behavior. David Sandler patterned his selling system after the compartments of a submarine. Each step of the selling system mirrored a submarine's compartments; each must be traversed in the proper order to move through the sales process.

The steps of the Sandler Submarine are:

- **Bonding & Rapport:** Building a relationship by developing a way to communicate effectively with the prospect and building trust.

- **Up-Front Contracts:** Getting on the same page as the prospect by setting expectations and ensuring an outcome to each sales call.

- **Pain:** Finding the prospect's reason to buy and gaining a commitment to resolve any issues keeping the prospect from greater success.

- **Budget:** Determining what the prospects are willing and able to invest to fix their pain.

- **Decision:** Working with the prospect's process to make a decision on your product or service.

- **Fulfillment:** Matching solutions to each pain uncovered during the sales process.

- **Post-Sell:** Dealing with "buyer's remorse" and blocking competitors from reopening a sale that has closed.

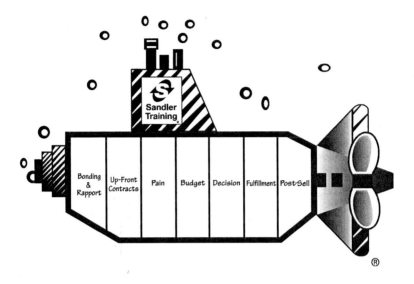

WHERE ARE THEY RIGHT NOW?

The effective coach recognizes the level of acceptance, openness, and commitment to success each individual salesperson brings to the coaching session. Specifically, the coach gauges the salesperson's current level of commitment to implementing the Sandler Selling System. With each new salesperson, the coach first asks, "Where is this person right now?" It should go without saying that the effective coach is just as committed to the Sandler principles as the salesperson is—and is committed, too, to some core assumptions about effective management.

Among these assumptions is the idea that coaching is quite different from the other three functions of the sales manager. For one thing, it is impossible to coach in a group setting, such as a weekly sales meeting. Coaching always takes place in a one-on-one environment and is customized to the salesperson's learning style and individual needs.

For another thing, coaching is not about particular targets. Many managers fail in the coaching role because they focus on achieving desired numerical results instead of supporting significant behavior modification and growth. The manager acting effectively as a coach shifts away from the need to direct change and fix problems and focuses instead on helping the salesperson discover for himself a more effective way to act in the selling situation.

BEGIN AT THE BEGINNING

Each coaching session begins with two assessments: one by the person to be coached, called the self-assessment, and the other by the coach, designated as the coaching assessment. You'll learn more about these a little later on in the book.

Just as important as the assessments is an understanding of the nature of the coaching meetings. The most successful coaches help salespeople understand that coaching is a developmental process. It's designed to help the salesperson become a better person, not just a more productive worker.

THE TIMING CHALLENGE

Coaching must be consistently scheduled at regular intervals for it to be effective and deliver the desired results.

Many managers fail because they view coaching as an event

designed to correct some specific, narrowly defined problem and/ or achieve a particular numerical result. Instead, the goal of coaching is continuous growth by the salesperson over a measured period of time. Managers who believe they don't have the time in their crowded schedule for coaching typically focus on micromanaging sales quotas and selling activity. They only have one-on-one meetings with the salesperson for short-term emergencies rather than for long-term changes to patterns of interaction.

SANDLER COACHING INSIGHT

The goal of coaching is continuous growth by the salesperson over a measured period of time.

The successful coach has studied Sandler's Identity/Role Theory, understands the impact of self-worth on achievement, and helps salespeople maintain a strong Identity and belief in self while at the same time helping them improve Role performance.

If the concepts of Identity and Role are new to you, here's a brief overview. The Sandler concept of self-worth is based on the separation of Identity (who you are) and Role (what you do). Role performance is based on the behavior salespeople perform in order to be successful in their jobs. Furthermore, coaching focuses on helping salespeople further develop their strengths and overcome blind spots that form unproductive patterns. This kind of relationship unfolds not in one or two intense crisis sessions but through consistent interaction—ideally, every two weeks.

A SAFE ENVIRONMENT

Coaching must take place in a safe environment in which the coach and salesperson have the ability to share open, honest, fact-based feedback. Many managers confuse coaching with training. They view the coaching process as a way to "fix" issues negatively impacting the bottom line, often creating an environment that feels unsafe for the salesperson. (How do you feel when someone tries to fix you?)

Training is the imparting of new skills. Coaching, on the other hand, is a way of empowering salespeople to use their existing skill set more effectively in the context of the sales process and thus achieve greater success.

Like good sales calls, coaching sessions require a strong up-front contract in which participants develop and agree to a meaningful agenda. This agenda becomes the focus of the session. A time contract specifying the duration of the meeting is critical for the initial session as well as all succeeding sessions.

A SPECIAL NOTE ABOUT UP-FRONT CONTRACTS

All Sandler trainers understand the power of the up-front contract in the sales process. This is equally important in the coaching process. In coaching, an up-front contract covers the timeframe for the session, the timing of the follow-up sessions, and the salesperson's agenda and coaching methodology. Lastly, the up-front contract ensures there are actionable next steps as well as accountability on the part of both salesperson and coach.

? **WHAT DOES IT MEAN?**

● Newcomers to the Sandler Selling System may ask, "What is an **up-front contract**?" The objective and intended outcome of a coaching discussion, the time element, and the role each party will play in reaching the intended outcome should all be agreed on in advance—preferably when the meeting is scheduled—and reviewed and reconfirmed at the beginning of the meeting.

Agreeing in advance about the topics for discussion, as well as what information will be provided and by whom, ensures against both misunderstandings and unfulfilled expectations. By establishing an objective for the interaction, the topics to be discussed, and the intended outcome, along with any associated next steps, this up-front contract not only sets the direction and tone of the discussion, but also provides a guidepost for getting the conversation back on track should it begin to wander off course. It establishes benchmarks by which to measure the progress made during the meeting as well.

Here is an example of an up-front contract between the coach and salesperson.

Coach: Thanks for taking the time to meet today. This session will take approximately forty-five minutes. I have blocked the time so we won't have any interruptions. During the session we will focus on prospecting since you seem to be struggling in that area. We will both contribute thoughts on ways to improve your effectiveness in this key area and at the end develop some action steps for you to perform between this session and the next one. Are you comfortable spending our time this way?

Salesperson: Yes, I am.

Coach: Is there anything you'd like to add?

Salesperson: I'm struggling with developing a consistent prospecting methodology so I avoid working on it. Additionally, I have trouble dealing with the constant rejection I face on the phone.

Coach: I'll add those to the agenda, and we can deal with those issues during the session.

The salesperson must take accountability for executing any new behaviors discussed in the coaching session, and these actions should be specifically summed up at the session's end.

SANDLER COACHING INSIGHT

The coaching up-front contract incorporates:
- Purpose or goal
- Time: meeting and follow up
- Salesperson/coach agenda
- Coach's role and process
- Accountability and next steps

DISCOVERY-BASED THINKING

Coaching salespeople requires discovery-based thinking. In this kind of thinking, salespeople open their minds and determine their own solutions to any problems. The best coaching sessions involve the salesperson discovering new ways to modify existing behavior to achieve the desired outcome. This is impossible when the salesperson does not feel safe.

> ## SANDLER COACHING INSIGHT
>
> Coaching is not an event; rather, it's a process of ongoing discovery. Often, it fails because it is seen as a "one and done" session where change is supposed to take place instantaneously.

THREE CRITICAL ELEMENTS

The three critical elements to understand during each coaching session are **what**, **reason**, and **importance**. By this I mean the shared purpose of the coaching session (the what), why it is necessary to achieve the mutually agreed-upon goal (the reason), and the real-world impact the accomplishment will have for the salesperson (the importance).

Successful coaches are able to establish all three early in coaching relationships and to measure the level of trust the salespeople have in them. Trust is a key factor driving success and can be measured using the same symbols used in the Olympics: gold, silver, and bronze.

Gold level trust is achieved over time. This must be the coach's ultimate goal. The most productive coaching sessions involve the highest level of trust between participants. This high level of trust fosters internal exploration through openness and vulnerability and speeds growth and development. Silver level trust is that which exists when there is the potential for growth, but there is not yet complete openness and vulnerability. Bronze level trust is that which exists when there are no known barriers to constructive interaction, but the coaching relationship has only just begun.

STRATEGIC VS. TACTICAL COACHING

Most successful coaches conduct two forms of coaching sessions: **strategic** and **tactical**. Strategic coaching focuses on helping salespeople plan for success. Tactical coaching helps them understand the skills and execution traps preventing them from greater success. Note that tactical coaching does not equate to, "Here, watch me do it!"

In both strategic and tactical coaching, the number one focus of the coach is to ask critical questions in order to help the participant fully understand the issues driving the coaching session.

Advanced questioning skills are key to successful strategic and tactical coaching sessions. They help the coach avoid the "telling/fixing" trap. The coach's best friend is active listening. The simple query, "Tell me more," gets the information ball rolling and allows the participant to "play a movie" of the events leading up to the session.

? WHAT DOES IT MEAN?

Active listening is the process of reflecting back to the speaker the message you heard in order to confirm or correct your understanding. It can be accomplished by summarizing the speaker's message and asking for confirmation or clarification as needed. Active listening not only facilitates effective communication, but it also enhances rapport.

The Sandler concepts of **reversing** (answering a question with a question) as well as strip-lining (presenting an idea that is the opposite of the one your conversational partner expects to hear) play significant roles in gathering the information needed to help the participant achieve the desired strategic or tactical outcome. This kind of engagement keeps the focus on the salesperson's understanding of the situation. It is important for the coach to listen without prejudice and judgment in order to reflect back to the salesperson what is being said accurately. The coach must block predetermined opinions about the situation or salesperson since they will skew the results of the session.

THE GAME PLAN

Let's consider some basic ground rules for effective coaching. One of these is that every coaching session, without exception, should have a strategy or game plan designed to achieve a certain desired result. Coaching fails when one or both participants enter into the session with no goal or plan for success. While a good conversation may well be the result of an unplanned session and both parties may end up "feeling good," nothing meaningful or lasting will have been accomplished.

Prior to the start of coaching the salesperson must have a clear understanding of what success in the position looks like. Often a gap analysis—a close examination of where the salesperson is now compared to where he wants to be—can be helpful. The top ten behaviors the salesperson must perform in order to be successful is also a good starting point. Each of these behaviors should have a clear expectation of performance associated with it. These behaviors are defined by analyzing success factors, activity, and key performance indicators (see Chapter Two).

Below, you'll find a list of the typical top ten sales behaviors for field salespeople—a list we'll be referencing often in this book. (Notice that the list can be considered either a list of **skills**—that which is learned—or a list of **behaviors**—that which is executed during the course of the selling day—depending on which aspect the coach chooses to emphasize.) Identifying strategies for measurable improvement in one of these ten areas is a good goal for just about any coaching session.

1. **Lead generation:** Prospecting, the number one behavior that drives all the others.

2. **Building relationships:** Establishing a strong, open relationship based on trust.

3. **Qualifying opportunity:** Determining a reason to do business.

4. **Making presentations:** Presenting solutions to the prospect's problems.

5. **Servicing customers:** Delivering superior customer satisfaction.

6. **Account management:** Maximizing business in each account.

7. **Territory development:** Building a strategy to grow the territory.

8. **Building a Cookbook for Success:** Establishing productive sales activity.

9. **Continuous education:** Developing ongoing product, market, and sales knowledge.

10. **Execution of the Sandler Selling System:** Mastering the sales process.

THE PLEASURE PRINCIPLE

Most salespeople are motivated by the pleasure principle. They want to attain a goal—owning a home outright, for instance—the attainment of which is expected to bring about pleasure and positive feelings in their life. This common dynamic makes salespeople quite easy to coach once the reward is determined. If you don't know what reward will deliver the pleasure, however, you're flying blind.

The pleasure principle focuses on the reward that salespeople receive for the behavior they perform. The problem is that the pursuit of the reward often has roadblocks associated with it. In these situations, the salesperson is similar to a machine that has a pebble in one of its cogs—a pebble that won't allow it to operate properly. Once the pebble is removed, the machine performs as it was designed. By the way, the same applies to the salesperson who has a behavior or belief impeding progress. Once the blockage is removed, the salesperson is free to pursue the goal that will deliver pleasure—and perform to the maximum level of execution.

WHY INVEST TIME IN COACHING?

Sales managers typically spend less than 10% of their time coaching salespeople and 90% of their time managing sales metrics. They view the formal performance review process as the number one form of coaching. They supplement this meeting with casual motivational conversations. Unfortunately coaching is seen as an added burden on their already full workload, so they focus their time on problem-solving activities.

In reality, coaching only adds to the manager's workload in the beginning. Yes, it takes time to gain traction with the process. However, in the long term coaching greatly reduces the managerial workload. It has a significant positive impact on sales force development and is a key factor for growing the sales team. Coaching allows you to decipher each salesperson's personal performance code.

Let me explain why a more effective coaching routine is a net productivity gain for virtually every sales manager. Too many salespeople view their sales manager as the CPS: Chief Problem Solver. This focus on problem-solving prevents sales managers from fulfilling their true mission of developing the sales team. Unfortunately, managers usually accept this honorary title and consider it part of their formal job description. They spend a majority of their time focusing on dealing with operational and financial issues, leaving them little or no time to develop the individual members of the team. (A side note: Managers who ask the question, "How would you solve this problem if I weren't here?" find their salespeople usually have the answers and could act on their own. "Learned helplessness" prevents them from doing so.)

FIVE REASONS FOR EFFECTIVE COACHING

Here are the top five reasons high-performing companies build coaching into their sales culture:

1. Coaching develops proficiency, self-sufficiency, and time competency in salespeople. These three areas focus on the better usage of existing skills, improved competence during their sales calls, and ensuring time is an asset, not a liability.
2. Coaching is a sign of corporate investment and support, which are significant contributors to attracting and retaining sales superstars.
3. Coaching is extremely important in a salesperson's career development and overall job satisfaction rating.
4. Coaching impacts the ego, confidence, and self-worth of the sales team and helps drive independent growth.
5. Coaching enhances the professional relationship between

manager and salesperson and develops a healthy, effective work relationship.

My challenge to you is simple. Begin to look at coaching as a developmental tool that helps you be a better manager. Coaching frees up your day by allowing you to escape from the "warden" mentality—and focus on truly leading your sales team strategically.

THE RELATIONSHIP BETWEEN COACHING AND PERFORMANCE

Performance coaching involves a dialogue between a trusted manager and willing salesperson, designed to impact both the salesperson's wellbeing (who they are) and personal performance (what they do). In Sandler terms, this involves working on the salesperson's intrinsic Identity as well as external Role. It is impossible for a salesperson to achieve the highest level of performance unless these two critical sides of self-worth are addressed.

SANDLER COACHING INSIGHT

The coach's job is to help salespeople become the best possible version of themselves.

As I mentioned earlier, the performance coaching process is driven by the productive agenda mutually set by the coach and salesperson. The point bears repeating: This agenda must be clear and must receive full agreement by both parties before each session begins. Not only that: This agenda must have clear expectations as well as a defined structure and methodology that allows participants to achieve the goal.

Effective coaching sessions are focused on facilitating the discoveries the salesperson will make. These discoveries must be driven, not by the manager's desire to impart best practices, but by the salesperson's personal commitment to work toward reaching full potential. The ability to focus on potential is the key to the performance coaching relationship.

Some example areas of performance coaching are: "next level" goal setting; career-pathing; belief examination and changing; behavior modification; recovering from personal and professional setbacks; removing subconscious roadblocks, etc. Salespeople who benefit most from the coaching experience are driven to be the best and open to change. They also are serial goal-setters and personally introspective. High-performance coaching helps salespeople explore their internal motivation as well as the external roadblocks that keep them from greater success. It focuses on supporting their current position in life and challenging them to grow beyond it.

THE BIG PICTURE OF COACHING

Every salesperson should develop a professional vision that guides behavioral choices and provides direction for decision making. This vision must include personal aspirations as well as values. The coach must understand the professional vision and relate the sales-person's goals to the vision throughout the course of the coaching sessions. This is precisely the process I followed with Barbara. It's the process that led not only to her breakthrough, but to countless breakthroughs experienced by sales professionals in other fields.

As mentioned earlier, the most effective coaching strategies begin with the creation of a success profile clearly delineating behavior the salesperson must perform in order to be consid-ered successful in the job. (If you don't have such a profile, you may want to use the list of top ten behaviors mentioned earlier in this chapter as a starting point.) Once this profile is clear in both the coach's and salesperson's mind, the coach's function is to work with the salesperson on ways to consistently improve per-formance. The coach does this by developing a plan for a series of sessions focused on identifying specific behavioral opportunities for growth and by asking good questions.

ELEMENTS OF A SUCCESSFUL COACHING STRATEGY

There are three critical elements to creating a successful coaching strategy: the plan, the environment, and the methodology.

The coaching plan should be well thought out. I have to emphasize once again that a good session can't possibly be con-ducted in a "wing it" fashion. Coaching salespeople for higher performance is a process, not an event. Each succeeding coaching session must build off the previous one so the salesperson feels the velocity of change. Consistent follow up is critical to sustaining the levels of growth achieved in the prior sessions.

The emotional environment for the sessions must be open, honest and non-judgmental. For many managers, this is a major challenge. There are Three P's of Trust associated with the coaching environment: potency, permission, and protection. (These are described in detail in Chapter Five.) Effective coaches resist any tendency to position themselves as authority figures, so that the salespeople assume full potency within their own career. Additionally, coaches give the salespeople permission to speak freely and provide protection from any reprisal from the ideas exchanged. This assurance allows each person the freedom to express all pertinent thoughts.

The methodology is the roadmap. It must be abundantly clear to both the manager and the salesperson. This eliminates mindreading as a prerequisite for participating in the sessions. Salespeople must clearly see the roadmap by which a coach aids them in achieving their goals.

WHAT DRIVES THE SESSION?

The salesperson's goals must drive all the coaching sessions. It's virtually impossible to effectively coach a salesperson who is not 100% committed to clearly identified personal goals. Without goals, there is nothing driving the salesperson to take action.

When developing a coaching strategy, it is important to have salespeople clearly spell out the goals as well as explain why the goals have personal meaning for them. Then come the steps of building accountability and an action plan, followed by the equally important step of making sure salespeople reward themselves for all progress made. Too many salespeople wait until they have achieved the ultimate goal before they celebrate. Mini-celebrations along the way provide the jet fuel necessary for continued effort.

Salespeople who develop a personal vision to act as a beacon guiding their direction and their daily choices are the ones who experience the greatest success. This vision typically includes aspirations as well as values and informs behavioral decisions that drive performance improvement. Effective coaches support the identification and expression of this vision. Barb's vision, for example, was to create a certain kind of company, one that attracted the very best customers and team members.

WHY MANAGERS FAIL AT COACHING

Every manager has the ability to develop the skills necessary to be a great coach. However, many lack the willingness to commit to the action plan necessary to help their own salespeople grow and develop. This book is meant to help you develop and execute such an action plan.

In my experience, a majority of coaches merely give lip service and a halfhearted effort to the coaching process. They default to being supervisors, assuming that this will help the members of their sales team achieve success. They use their authority as a club, imagining that they are pushing people toward success. Instead, they are creating a hostage mentality within their sales force. In this situation, salespeople focus on doing only what they are told, when they are told to do it—and they underperform.

Coaching takes a strong commitment by the manager to empower salespeople to grow. It creates a continuous learning environment, propelling salespeople past self-imposed barriers.

THE MOST COMMON TRAPS

Here are some common traps managers fall into that prevent them from being better coaches.

Unclear objectives for the coaching session. Each coaching session must have a solid, meaningful agenda that both parties agree to achieve. Salespeople must have an emotional tie to the positive impact that completing the agenda will have on them.

Poor follow up on the session. Unless the coach and the salesperson commit to the necessary follow up, the session will not be successful. This commitment has to be unconditional. It should have intermediate review points to make sure the salesperson stays on track.

Lack of trust. Meaningful growth cannot occur in the absence of trust. If there is not a gold or silver level of trust between manager and salesperson at the end of the first meeting, the coach should first explore why there is an absence of trust. It is important to get all the relevant issues on the table in order to ensure that a strong level of trust is present, since it allows the openness necessary for coaching intimacy.

Too much time spent fixing. Managers who habitually

respond with, "Here's what I would do if I were you," or any variation, are not coaching. In such situations, the salesperson proceeds
to do only what the manager says to do, and significant growth
opportunities are lost.

Too much time spent telling. Some managers feel they have
to have all the answers so they are constantly telling their salespeople what to do. Instead, managers must develop a pattern of
strategic questioning designed to make the salesperson open up,
think differently, and speak freely.

Impatience if results take too long. The sales profession
focuses intensely on achieving bottom-line results. Time is of
the essence in achieving those results, so it's not surprising that
managers get impatient. Successful coaching sessions are based on
the idea that becoming a great salesperson is a marathon, not a
sprint. Marathon runners understand that it is important to pace
themselves and to watch the mile markers on the side of the road
in order to create the proper pace. Sprinters, on the other hand,
are more focused on running the race as fast as they can. The best
coaches have the patience of a marathoner, and they encourage
their salespeople to think the same way.

Coaching all salespeople the same way. Each salesperson is
unique. Coaching is not accomplished in a one-size-fits-all world,
and every coaching session requires a customized approach based
on knowledge of the salesperson's specific needs. Assessments can
provide great coaching roadmaps to guide the deep understanding necessary for success.

Successful coaches view coaching as an art form as well as a science. They adhere to a defined methodology and personalize that methodology to fit the individual needs of a specific salesperson. The chapters that follow are meant to help you do just that.

SANDLER COACHING RULES

- Benchmark the salesperson's current skill set before the coaching process begins.
- Keep the salesperson's Identity strong while you improve the Role.
- Develop a coaching up-front contract, and personalize a strategy for each session.
- Establish a high level of trust and openness with the salesperson.
- Remember that coaching is similar to running a marathon, since it requires a strong commitment to "go the distance."

CHAPTER TWO

Developing the Coach's Mindset

OVERVIEW

- "Seek first to understand"
- The attributes of a successful coach
- The importance of coaching awareness and self-worth
- Purpose, awareness, and behavior

In this chapter, you will gain a full understanding of the depth of the issues facing the salesperson. By doing this, you can eliminate any predetermined notions about the salesperson and focus on the behavioral changes necessary for success.

"SEEK FIRST TO UNDERSTAND"

Stephen Covey's famous book—you know which one I mean—outlines the seven habits of the elite group he identifies as "highly effective people." His fifth habit is my favorite: "Seek first to understand." This sound advice concisely describes the habitual approach of highly effective sales coaches. If I had to boil this book down to a single sentence, that's the one I would choose.

The coach's job is indeed to understand the true depth and full scope of the issues keeping a salesperson from attaining greater success. Once the coach fully understands these issues, the main job becomes twofold: helping the salesperson focus on all the growth options available, and helping the salesperson deal with the specific beliefs preventing full attainment of personal potential.

None of this is easy or fast, and all of it is unique to the individual being coached. This is why the most effective coaches seek first to understand the salesperson as a person. Only by building on this kind of understanding can the coach encourage broader thinking on the part of the salesperson and a deeper examination of the traditional beliefs preventing constructive, sustainable changes in behavior.

ALEX'S STORY

Alex is a nine-year veteran salesperson who has struggled throughout his career with strong-willed prospects who are eager to assume control of the sales process. This situation has left Alex largely ineffective in his sales role, since he is only able to close the prospects who create a friendly atmosphere and appear to like him. He feels he should take his time with these prospects, get to know them, and eventually reach a point where everyone feels comfortable agreeing to do business.

Around the office, Alex always appears to be busy, so his manager Keiko is impressed with his work ethic. Yet Alex consistently fails to hit the modest performance targets he and Keiko have set together. Prospects always seem to show up in his weekly report with no resolution in sight. His deals are perpetually pending.

I could tell Keiko was frustrated with this pattern. She felt Alex could be her top performer if even half of his "perpetually pending" prospects ever closed. Keiko's assessment of the problem was a common one: She wanted me to "teach Alex to be a better closer." It seemed obvious to Keiko that what Alex needed was a heaping extra helping of sales training.

I wasn't so sure. My analysis of the situation suggested that Alex had the skills and the knowledge of the Sandler system necessary to close more business. However, his inability to deal with difficult prospects prevented him from using these skills during his sales calls.

Alex saw any disagreement with a prospect as conflict and shied away from that conflict because it made him uncomfortable. Not only that, he shied away from perceived conflicts with Keiko for precisely the same reason. Yet, his relationship with his boss was growing more and more strained. Something had to give.

Some background is in order here. Alex is a middle child who was brought up with a high need for approval. The problem wasn't that he hadn't been trained in the Sandler process. The problem was his internalized beliefs were preventing him from using sales techniques that he thought might make his prospects not like him.

During our coaching sessions, Alex and I explored his "life script"—his habitual way of looking at himself and the world— and the impact it was having on his selling success. Dealing with these unspoken issues helped Alex free himself from the thoughts and assumptions that were holding his performance hostage.

I used the doctor/patient analogy with Alex to help him see the real issue. If he were a doctor and a patient showed up in his office with back pain, he wouldn't treat the back pain until he was sure of the cause—no matter how strong a personality the patient had. Selling, I suggested, must be seen in the same light. You cannot prescribe a solution to a prospect's problem until you understand the depth of the issue—no matter what aggressive traits the prospect may be portraying.

Once Alex got his heart into this analogy, his way of looking at his work changed. So did his behavior—and so did his sales results—and so did his relationship with his manager Keiko.

WHAT ARE THE SELF-LIMITING BELIEFS?

The effective sales coach deals directly with the self-limiting thoughts in the salesperson's head that are preventing the execution of new, higher-performing behaviors. Once the salesperson reflects inwardly and analyzes his own thinking, he can eliminate the excuse "I've always done it this way!" and focus on new behavioral possibilities never previously explored.

The effective coach's strategy for growth focuses on exploring new thoughts and behaviors that may be the exact opposite of current behavior patterns. Not only that, the coach finds the best course of action for a radical transformation of the salesperson's thought process. The change in thinking must take place first; otherwise, the change in behavior is impossible. If the salesperson cannot think oppositely from his current thought process, he will repeat the unproductive patterns and habits, thus creating (or worsening) a behavioral rut.

SPIN AND DENIAL

The effective coach helps the salesperson work through the shock associated with a selling behavior that has stopped delivering the expected results.

Many salespeople develop a kind of "spin cycle" to deal with the jolt that comes from sudden, unexpected failure, and a fair number of them move into denial: "This can't be happening to me." They are, however, unaware of this shock/denial cycle so they become frustrated, unmotivated, and begin blaming their prospects (or management, administrative support, or others) for their lack of success.

The Sandler Coaching System outlined in this book is designed to create new beliefs and behavioral modification by shifting the salesperson out of the cycle of shock and denial into the realm of experimentation and acceptance. Coaching helps the salesperson explore new ways of dealing with traditional sales problems presented in the course of the buyer/seller relationship and form more productive, although initially less comfortable, behavior patterns. This requires the salesperson to have a high degree of openness to change as well as a willingness to be uncomfortable when implementing these changes.

"I'm good at being uncomfortable." —Fiona Apple

THE NINE ATTRIBUTES OF AN EFFECTIVE COACH

The successful coach has the ability to view the coaching process as both a science and an art form. Coaching is akin to science in the sense that it follows a repeatable process with clearly defined steps that achieve the desired result. While the science is rooted in the coaching process, the art form of coaching is fueled by open-ended curiosity and the ability to notice and follow one's intuition—traits that great poets, painters, writers, and composers bring to any successful project. The most effective coaches have a high degree of curiosity driving the need to fully explore all sides of an issue. Over time, great coaches also develop strong intuition based on their many past coaching experiences.

Here are nine attributes an effective coach possesses:

1. **High self-awareness:** The coach must have a high degree of self-awareness and use this to maintain an objective perspective during the coaching process.

2. **Balanced focus:** The coach must explore the mix of personal and professional issues affecting the salesperson's performance and must understand that these combined issues may have a positive or negative impact on sales performance.

3. **Ability to solve problems:** The coach must utilize the ability to analyze each salesperson and determine the true genesis of the problem, separating it from unrelated areas that might cause sidetracking.

4. **Sincere interest and desire to help:** The coach must be sincerely interested in helping the salesperson develop as a person. The coach must not view the coaching session as a perfunctory part of the role.

5. **Nurturing and nonjudgmental feedback skills:** The coach must focus on giving neutral, nonjudgmental feedback. (Such feedback comes from the Nurturing Parent and Adult ego states; you'll learn more about these ego states in Chapter Five.) This focus protects the self-worth of the salesperson and enables acceptance of the feedback.

6. **Strategic thinking skills:** The coach focuses on the big picture and works through issues strategically. This big-picture approach helps the salesperson broaden his thinking and explore all the available options.

❓ WHAT DOES IT MEAN?

Emotional detachment: The coach must maintain objectivity and ensure emotionally sensitive issues aren't transferred from the salesperson to the coach. This objectivity allows the coach to provide honest insight and ask difficult questions with respect and integrity.

7. **Openness to new ideas and approaches:** The coach displays openness during the coaching sessions and does not steer salespeople toward the coach's desired result. This allows salespeople to take ownership of their own ideas and ensures personal acceptance and ownership of all new behaviors.

8. **Trustworthiness:** The coach earns a high degree of trust and recognizes the need to be professionally vulnerable in order to create the right atmosphere for the coaching session. Trust is only built over time, and it has to be continuously strengthened—or it will decay. As a general rule, people don't trust coaches who show zero vulnerability.

9. **Questioning and listening skills:** The coach asks the difficult questions and then listens with both ears to the responses. The coach is at ease with any discomfort caused by questions asked as part of the coaching process. Only the salesperson's honest answers to these tough questions will drive growth. Additionally, the coach recognizes that the salesperson is only growing in understanding when responding—not when the coach is talking.

These important coaching attributes are developed over time. Unfortunately, they are rarely present when the manager first enters the coaching arena.

THE IMPORTANCE OF COACHING AWARENESS AND SELF-WORTH

It is difficult to coach a salesperson who has low self-awareness. Such a salesperson is always externalizing his problems and rarely if ever taking personal responsibility. The challenge faced by the coach working with someone with low self-awareness is to ask thoughtful questions that will help the salesperson look internally for answers. This internal examination helps the salesperson understand the positive or negative role his beliefs, habits, and life script play. This understanding is crucial in determining the best solution to any problem the salesperson faces. An effective coach serves as a subtle role model for the salesperson in the area of personal self-awareness.

Self-worth is equally important. The effective coach always stays focused on the best course of action for the salesperson. The coaching session should be designed to provide a roadmap to achieve this result. The coach must be careful, however, not to inject himself into the salesperson's picture, and this requires a strong sense of self-worth on the coach's part.

The concept of self-worth and its impact on success are critical components of Sandler sales training, so let's look at those issues in depth now. Self-worth, as described by David Sandler, is derived from the complex blending of who you are (your Identity) and what you do (your Role). If coaches focus too much on the Role (which is what usually happens with an inexperienced coach)—if how salespeople perform within that Role is all that is ever discussed—they will miss the critical fact that salespeople can only perform in their Role to the degree that they believe in themselves.

Successful coaches understand the importance of a strong Identity. They know that a strong Identity helps the salesperson make the difficult changes necessary for improved performance. Here again, the effective sales coach's own sense of self-worth serves as a subtle, but motivating, role model.

GOALS AND THE RULE OF THREE AND TWO

The process of setting meaningful personal goals is one of the keys to helping the salesperson maintain a strong sense of self-worth. In the coaching session, the Rule of Three and Two keeps the salesperson's self-worth balanced. Simply stated, the Rule of Three and Two suggests that the salesperson focus weekly on developing three professional goals and two personal goals to commit to achieving each week. The three professional goals are designed to improve Role performance, while the two personal goals are designed to strengthen Identity and belief in oneself.

Goal setting is an important driver of success; however, in my experience, only 20% of salespeople are goal setters and fully committed to the process. Most lower performers set goals only because they are told to do so or are occasionally motivated to set goals and lose interest soon after they are set. The 20% who are 100% committed to the goal-setting process view goal achievement to be as necessary as the oxygen they breathe.

AN ENCOUNTER WITH DAVID SANDLER

In October 1994, when I began building my Sandler Training® business, I knew little about sales training and less about running a business. At the end of one particularly grueling day, I called the Sandler home office to speak with my coach. She surprised me by putting me on the phone with David Sandler himself, who happened to be passing by her office.

David asked how my business was going. I explained to him that it was a bit of a struggle at the moment. I was working 15-hour days trying to learn the Sandler Training material and develop solid business practices. He asked what I was doing for myself, and I explained I didn't have time for any of that. I knew I needed to throw myself into the business; I had committed to work on myself after the business had a strong foundation. There would be plenty of time to set aside for myself once my business was up and running.

In his most nurturing tone, David shocked me by saying, "Bill, I hate to be the one to tell you this, but you will fail miserably before that ever happens!" When I asked why, he said, "You're putting far too much pressure on your Role success. You will be extremely frustrated when success doesn't come as quickly as you thought it should. You need to work on keeping your belief in yourself strong while you're developing the skills necessary for success."

I was puzzled, but I sensed, in some deep part of myself, that he was right. That night, when I arrived home from yet another challenging day at the office, my wife Gayle and I went to the movies. The move playing was *A River Runs Through It*. The film, as you may know, is about fly-fishing (among other things), and it certainly piqued my interest. I began to think about fly-fishing as something I should try for myself.

The next day I went to the local fly shop and spent $39 on a beginner's fly-fishing rod and reel. Each morning, before I started my day, I went to the pond in front of my building to practice my casting. In the beginning, my casts were terrible and not likely to catch many fish. Even so, I kept at it.

Every morning, at 6:00 A.M. sharp, I repeated the ritual and found my casting technique improved with surprising speed. As my casting improved, so did my business!

Who could say why for sure? I didn't try to explain it to myself, beyond noticing that it seemed casting was a metaphor for the business success that I was about to achieve. One thing was certain: I was feeling better about myself. This internal feeling fueled confidence during my sales calls.

I went from casting in a pond to fishing small streams in Wisconsin on the weekends. I looked forward to learning as much as possible, in my spare time, about the art of fly-fishing. Today, 21 years later, I still use the sport as an integral part of my personal development. This seemingly unrelated activity bolstered my confidence and strengthened my Identity—which translated into stronger Role performance. That's a lesson I never forgot.

ROLE FAILURE

A decay in the salesperson's Identity typically drives Role failure. If the salesperson's Identity doesn't remain strong, there is no anchor to stop the downward spiral caused by occasional (and, let's face it, inevitable) Role failure. The coach must continuously be on the lookout for any beliefs that devalue the salesperson's self-worth and must also remember to serve as a constant role model for a healthy personal identity.

PURPOSE, AWARENESS, AND BEHAVIOR

Every effective coaching session with a salesperson focuses on three main elements: purpose, awareness, and behavior. Without this concentration, the session becomes too conversational and, in the end, no sustainable growth occurs, despite both parties feeling "positive" about the session.

Let's look at each of these elements in turn.

Purpose

All effective coaching sessions set clear long-term and short-term goals. The long-term goals typically focus on behavioral modification over a 90-day period and are designed to develop sustainable habits. These goals are strategic in nature, and long-term planning is necessary in order to accomplish them. Short-term goals, by contrast, make an immediate positive impact and help create a "success track," allowing the salesperson to build on each previous accomplishment. Marathon runners, after all, don't simply get out of bed one morning and decide to run 26.2 miles without ever having done so before. Typically, the marathoner begins by running much shorter races to build stamina and endurance. Gradually these shorter races become longer and longer until the marathoner has achieved the ability to run the full race. Short-term goals for the salesperson accomplish the same thing. Achievement of these goals begins to build traction, and the positive behavior modification associated with them creates the path toward achievement of the long-term goal.

A verbal contract between the coach and the salesperson is a critical part of accomplishing the purpose identified for the session. This is a binding agreement in which mutual expectations are established and defined by coach and salesperson that determine a specific outcome for the session before the session begins in earnest.

Awareness

The effective coach develops heightened awareness in three important areas: **self-awareness**, **situational awareness**, and **experiential awareness**.

Coaches themselves should be introspective and possess a high level of personal self-awareness. As a result, they make the conscious effort to eliminate internal biases or prejudicial judgments based on prior coaching sessions. Such biases and judgments may subliminally influence the coaching session. For example, coaches may treat Millennial salespeople the same as they would Baby Boomers because they themselves happen to be Baby Boomers. This thought bias, if unchecked, might put the Millennial salespeople at a significant disadvantage since they have skills and characteristics that make it advisable for a coach to treat them differently than members of the Baby-Boom generation. For instance, their comfort level with technology and social media is likely to be much higher than that of Baby Boomers. This trait of Millennials could be an asset, but only if it's recognized and maximized.

The coach must also develop situational awareness. This kind of awareness fosters a 360-degree look at all the surrounding factors that could possibly affect the session. For example, a salesperson who is under pressure to perform at a higher level will act differently in a coaching session than a salesperson who is 25% ahead of quota. The coach has to understand these kinds of pressures and adjust accordingly, since they can have a major impact on the coaching environment.

Lastly, the coach needs experiential awareness. This helps the coach become aware of the many experiences—recent, in the distant past, or somewhere in between—that can influence the outcome of the session. For example, a salesperson who feels he has been treated unfairly by a manager in a prior sales job may assume that the same mistreatment will be the norm in his new company. This experience will prevent the salesperson from being as open and vulnerable as necessary for the session to be successful. Effective coaches can overcome this obstacle—but only if they know what is going on.

Behavior

The effective coach helps the salesperson understand the direct link between more effective behaviors and greater success in the job. If this understanding isn't clear in the salesperson's mind when he is in a pressure-filled situation (such as a sales call), the salesperson will revert to familiar, lower-performing behavior as a comfort zone.

SANDLER COACHING INSIGHT

High-performing coaches understand the difference between **effective** behavior and **efficient** behavior and find a way to share this understanding with their salespeople. Effective behavior delivers the desired result every time it is used. Efficient behavior is simply the easiest perceived route to the goal. Too many times salespeople resort to efficient or expedient behavior since, in their mind, this appears to be the more direct route to success. Effective behavior, on the other hand, may take more time and effort, but it guarantees that the proper result is achieved.

MODIFYING BEHAVIOR

The measure of a coaching session's success is how much behavioral modification occurs as a result. A new behavioral approach, whether large or small, is the first step in the salesperson's progress toward higher performance. It requires a strong commitment by the salesperson to eliminate old habits, question outdated beliefs, and stretch the comfort zone far beyond any point it may have defined in the past.

There are two key questions the coach must be able to answer prior to any attempt to modify the salesperson's behavior:

1. Does this salesperson currently have the selling skills necessary to succeed?

2. Does this salesperson understand how to execute those skills in the context of the selling situation?

If the answer to either of these questions is "no," the problem lies with training and not coaching. In such a case, the coach (or someone) needs to deliver the relevant skills training prior to beginning the coaching process. (Recall that "trainer" is in the job description of the effective sales manager.) This point is worth emphasizing. No amount of coaching can compensate for a skill gap. The salesperson must be trained—or, in some cases, retrained—on the strategies and tactics of the Sandler Selling System in order to provide a baseline for professional growth.

On the other hand, if the answer to both questions is "yes," the salesperson's issue can be addressed in a series of coaching sessions designed to help the salesperson better apply the skills already acquired.

THE TOP TEN BEHAVIORS

High-performing salespeople understand and consistently execute the top ten behaviors necessary for success, which you read about in Chapter One. This list of behaviors has helped thousands of Sandler-trained salespeople benchmark and raise their performance. Here's the list once again. It's extremely important, which is why I'm asking you to take another look at it now.

1. **Lead generation:** Prospecting, the number one behavior that drives all the others.

2. **Building relationships:** Establishing a strong, open relationship based on trust.

3. **Qualifying opportunity:** Determining a reason to do business.

4. **Making presentations:** Presenting solutions to the prospect's problems.

5. **Servicing customers:** Delivering superior customer satisfaction.

6. **Account management:** Maximizing business in each account.

7. **Territory development:** Building a strategy to grow the territory.

8. **Building a Cookbook for Success:** Establishing productive sales activity.

9. **Continuous education:** Developing ongoing product, market, and sales knowledge.

10. **Execution of the Sandler Selling System:** Mastering the sales process.

Do salespeople report to you? If you're this far into the book, I'm assuming that some do. If that's the case, you face a question: How well does each individual salesperson perform in each one of these categories? The answer you offer should be specific to the person you are discussing—and it should be something you can express on a 1–10 scale.

The effective coach benchmarks the performance of each of these ten behaviors in order to determine whether or not they are being performed at acceptable levels by a specific salesperson. Use the following rating system to categorize the success of each behavior: a 7–10 rating is considered high performance, a 3–7 rating places the salesperson in the variable performance range, and finally a 1–3 rating equates to poor performance. Salespeople

---

? WHAT DOES IT MEAN?

● **Key performance indicators** (KPIs) are simply the results achieved by the performance of a certain behavior. Here is an example: Prospecting is a behavior performed on a weekly basis. A KPI for prospecting would be the actual number of first face-to-face appointments yielded by the performance of the behavior. Six first face-to-face meetings per week might be an indicator of acceptable behavioral performance, so six could be identified as the KPI of success. If a salesperson only delivers three first face-to-face meetings in a given week, he would be performing below KPI.

tend to skew their own self-ratings higher, so the coach must develop and measure specific key performance indicators to justify the rating.

After the coach has effectively rated each behavior based on current performance, it's time to consider three keywords associated with improving the execution of each: **more, better,** and **different**.

1. Does the salesperson need to perform **more** of the behavior in order to raise his performance?

2. Does the salesperson need to perform the behavior **better** to raise his performance?

3. Does the salesperson need to perform the behavior in a **different** way in order to raise his performance?

The coach must carefully analyze the salesperson's current level of execution and determine which of these keywords apply and when. This kind of assessment helps salespeople realize the control they have over their own ability to succeed.

Here's the main thing I want you to understand before you move on to the next chapter: If you aren't benchmarking the ten sales behaviors for field salespeople, or if you haven't identified measurable key performance indicators that support each of those behaviors, then you have no way to gauge growth within the selling role, and no reason to expect any performance improvement from the salespeople who report to you.

SANDLER COACHING RULES

- Work to understand fully the depth of the issues keeping the salesperson from greater success prior to the start of the coaching process.

- Focus on your own continuous development of the top nine attributes all coaches need in order to be successful.

- Protect the salesperson's Identity when helping improve Role performance.

- Remember that goals the salesperson is 100% committed to accomplishing are essential to success.

- Benchmark the top ten sales behaviors and apply the "more, better, different" analysis to improve performance.

CHAPTER THREE

Dealing with Change

OVERVIEW

- Willingness to change drives performance
- Transition vs. change
- The Sandler Success Triangle
- The 20/60/20 Rule

This chapter will explore how the salesperson accepts the need to change. Most salespeople are resistant to change and choose to remain stuck. The effective coach breaks through this comfort zone to help salespeople reach their potential for greater success.

WILLINGNESS TO CHANGE DRIVES PERFORMANCE

Being comfortable kills performance!

Most salespeople—indeed, most people—focus on behavior that is comfortable and shun behavior that creates discomfort, even though the discomfort is temporary and may drive higher performance. The fact is, growth and high performance resides on the other side of comfort. "Man's reach," the poet Robert Browning said, "should exceed his grasp." He meant, I think, what David Sandler meant: All of us have to stretch our beliefs and behaviors in order to succeed.

DIEGO'S STORY

All Sandler franchisees offer weekly sales training workshops called the President's Club. During these sales training sessions, salespeople—many of whom have personally paid to be in the program—learn to apply the Sandler strategies and tactics consistently, in order to gain greater success in their sales role.

I have trained and coached countless salespeople and business leaders in the course of my 20-plus years as a Sandler franchisee. I don't accept just anyone into my Sandler training and coaching program. Before I allow salespeople to enter my program, they must first qualify by taking a behavioral assessment in order to detail their current level of competency and commitment. I have had to disqualify approximately 400 salespeople who didn't meet the behavioral and commitment standards that are a prerequisite for improved selling success. Before disqualifying people, I always offer to meet with them to explain why they aren't going to be allowed to enter the President's Club sales training program. During that discussion, I provide some basic coaching so the disqualification isn't cold and impersonal. We typically discuss behavioral or commitment gaps, and I always recommend a personal course of action they can take to correct the problems I outline.

Why do I tell you this? Because there is a lesson to be learned in the numbers. Astonishingly, of the 400 salespeople I've disqualified, only five pushed back, challenged their disqualification, and committed to the behavioral modifications necessary to be included in the President's Club program. That proportion (400:5) shows how committed people are to staying within their comfort zone. Those who are willing to stretch themselves, feel the discomfort, and make productive changes really stand out.

I remember in particular a salesperson named Diego. Upon disqualification, he indignantly challenged me as to what, specifically, he had to do to be included in the program. I invested the coaching time with Diego due to his determination and created a detailed list of the top ten behaviors he would have to execute consistently and the five personal traits he would have to display in order to be reconsidered for the program. He asked if I would consider regular coaching as part of his growth in order to keep him on track as well as help clear any mental roadblocks he might encounter during these major changes he had to implement. I agreed.

Diego and I met every ten days or so for the next few months. At the end of each coaching session, he left with an action plan he committed to execute as proof of his worthiness to be in the program. Our meetings took place early in the morning so we didn't interrupt his selling cycle. We usually discussed the deeply rooted beliefs that were preventing him from executing the more difficult behaviors necessary for higher performance. The conviction Diego demonstrated, as well as his willingness to question his beliefs and implement change, had an immediate impact on his sales call results as well as his overall selling success. Six months later he asked to requalify in order to be included in the training program. I reevaluated him, using our behavioral assessment, and found that the picture had indeed changed radically, just as Diego had promised me it would. He was immediately accepted into the President's Club.

Diego's strong conviction to win entry to the program and his willingness to move beyond his personal comfort zone helped him develop new levels of competency as well as a high level of ambition and drive. He rose from the rank of 50 (in a sales force of 100) to the number 3 performer. Over the next year, while attending my President's Club training program, Diego demonstrated the continuous behavioral modification that yielded ongoing growth as well as providing a great example to the other trainees on what a salesperson with strong conviction can accomplish.

UNCONDITIONAL COMMITMENT

Diego's story serves as a shining example of how a salesperson who is unconditionally committed to accomplishing a goal and has the guts to challenge entrenched beliefs and behaviors can excel. It's sad to think that only five of the 400 who weren't allowed into the President's Club committed to making the changes necessary to take control of their careers, choosing not to live professional lives mired in mediocrity.

Change is not easy. The easy way is to avoid change at all costs. The successful coach learns to recognize those few who are willing to push back and move beyond their comfort zone.

TRANSITION VS. CHANGE

Most salespeople refuse to accept the need for change unless there is a catastrophic event causing them to think differently about their situation.

There's an old saying, popular among effective sales coaches: "Salespeople change only when the pain of remaining the same is greater than the pain involved in the change." Such changes generally do not happen overnight. My own experience suggests that, when change supports growth, it is not like a light switch that goes on and off; rather, it gradually transitions the salesperson to a new, more desired state.

Elisabeth Kübler-Ross pioneered the now-famous "five stages of grief" model to help individuals deal with personal trauma and bereavement. These five stages—denial, anger, bargaining, depression, and acceptance—are typically applied to those individuals dealing with death, dying, or catastrophic loss. I have translated the Kübler-Ross model into four "transition steps" that I utilize in the Sandler coaching process.

This transition model I consistently utilize in my coaching process involves four stages: denial, resistance, exploration, and commitment.

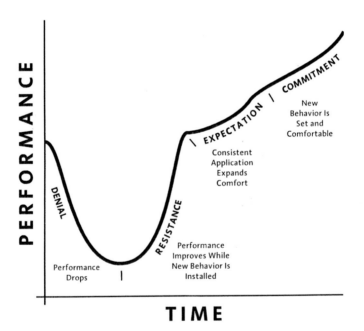

The key to helping salespeople move through these four stages involves understanding specifically where salespeople currently are and then helping them move through each stage to gain the momentum required to make the necessary changes.

Most traditional coaching fails because the coach expects the salesperson to walk in the door for the first session with the willingness to explore behavior (stage three) and engage in belief modification (stage four) at the outset. This approach ignores the reality that most salespeople deny (stage one) and resist (stage two) the need to change—regardless of what they may say to please the manager—and are actually complacent about the results they are currently achieving. In the early stages of coaching the coach must help the salesperson move from the stages of denial and resistance into the areas of exploration and commitment, which are the stages where true growth will happen.

SANDLER COACHING INSIGHT

Dr. Shad Helmstetter pioneered the field of self-talk as a way of understanding the impact of negative thoughts on our own success. Delving deeply into the thoughts people hold as true in their minds, he explored the possibility that as much as 80% of these thoughts are negative. Negative self-talk tells people that they can't or shouldn't attempt any behavior that may challenge a behavior they've grown used to. The salesperson who listens to this internal negative self-talk will typically shy away from executing any behavior that may result in discomfort. This reluctance to act differently potentially eliminates all uncomfortable activity that may drive growth and greater selling success. The effective coach is strong enough to challenge these internal thoughts and help the salesperson remove and replace them with self-talk that supports personal growth.

It's important to understand that all salespeople have an internal "streaming audio" of thoughts that plays and replays positive or negative self-talk.

These thoughts are repetitive, often unrecognizably subtle, and sometimes not at all in a person's best interests. Salespeople develop a selling style based on these thoughts that is either confident or unsure, either courageous or fearful, either committed or conditional. In order to develop higher performance, the effective coach addresses the salesperson's internal thought mechanism for what it is: a life script developed over time, full of motivators, de-motivators, and feelings of self-worth or self-limitation. Many of these internal thoughts are hardwired and impossible to change without help. They can, however, be effectively overcome by means of a series of conversations with a skilled coach.

Here are some steps that effective coaches teach salespeople to use to deal with persistent negative thoughts:

1. Clearly identify the specific negative thought you want to change. (For instance, "CEOs don't want to talk to me because I'm not important.")
2. Ask yourself, "What if the opposite were true?"
3. Close your eyes and visualize a positive thought associated with this opposite thinking. (For instance, "I add value to everyone I talk to, particularly CEOs, and they want to talk to me.")
4. Set a goal to build new, measurable behavior around the positive thought.
5. Execute and measure the behavior associated with this goal for twenty straight days.

SARA'S STORY

Sara was experiencing a rough patch in her sales career. She hadn't closed a sale in forty-five days, and she had begun to wonder whether she would ever close one again.

Her thoughts about selling were negative. Specifically, she thought, *This is not going to go well*, as she began conversations with her prospects. Predictably, the sales call ended badly, and her self-fulfilling prophecies came true. We discussed her situation and reprogrammed the negative thought as follows: *Sales is a game, and games have rules. I am in charge of the rules for my sales game.*

Her new behavior focused on using the Sandler Selling System as a chess player would. She listed the common objections her prospects used and developed a Sandler questioning strategy for each. Every time a prospect bullied her, she fell back and said, internally, *Not OK*, in just the same way she would if an opponent violated the rules of a chess game. In this way, her fear of her opponent's ability to fight was defused, which put a smile on her face. Her new goal focused on better pre-call planning and debriefing on her results with a peer. Her 20-day plan was designed to disqualify prospects rather than qualify them. That meant success was getting a *no* and "failure" was a *yes*—since she now understood and accepted that she was going to receive more *noes* then *yeses*.

These simple rule changes turned around Sara's attitude about her sales calls. She began attaining the success she deserved for her sales calls.

CHANGE THE RULES

The short exercise I shared and reinforced with Sara helped her subconscious mind reframe negative thoughts into positive actions that delivered an entirely different result.

Salespeople do have the ability to change their skill set, the way they use their skill set, their basic knowledge and understanding of the sales process, and their attitudes about selling. All they have to do is change the rules. Unfortunately, they usually don't do that on their own. Instead, they build comfort zones involving habits and patterns that hold their success hostage.

Change is perpetual. When the change is positive, it ought to be welcomed. Positive change can occur without disrupting business, even though the process of change can be unsettling.

THE SANDLER SUCCESS TRIANGLE

All salespeople fit into a behavior-belief model that places them in one of three categories: high, variable, or low performance. Positioning in one of these three categories is driven by the behavioral choices the salesperson makes as well as the internal beliefs the salesperson uses to support his choices. Just as bad choices place a salesperson in the low performing category, good choices and small positive goals that drive growth will move the salesperson up the scale into higher performance.

The Sandler Success Triangle is a good model for measuring the behavior contributing to a salesperson's inclusion in one

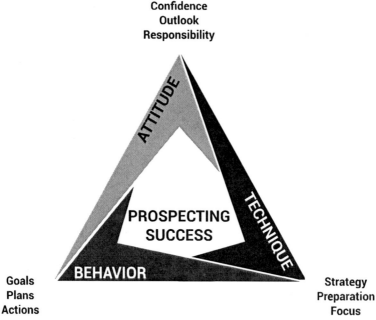

Confidence
Outlook
Responsibility

ATTITUDE

TECHNIQUE

PROSPECTING
SUCCESS

BEHAVIOR

Goals
Plans
Actions

Strategy
Preparation
Focus

of these categories. The three points on the triangle are behavior, attitude, and technique. They create a roadmap for high performance.

Behavior is the starting point for success. The salesperson should have a clear understanding of the top ten behaviors that must be consistently performed on a daily, weekly, and monthly basis. These behaviors must be executed with unconditional commitment. High performers understand the importance of turning these behaviors into specific measurable goals. After all, goals without plans are daydreams. Each behavior must have a clear strategic plan serving as a roadmap and must be placed on a calendar to monitor its delivery.

? ## WHAT DOES IT MEAN?

Behavior is what one actually does, day after day. If a salesperson doesn't do the day-to-day activities that support the sales process, it doesn't matter how many great techniques the coach passes along or what attitude the salesperson brings to the table. It's like a law of physics—you won't get results if you don't do the behaviors.

The next area of focus for high performers is **attitude,** which is a complex system of beliefs salespeople have about themselves, the selling process, the company that employs them, and the marketplace they serve. This belief system must support the behaviors required for success or the salesperson's attitude will result in doubt and conditional execution. Salespeople fail when their belief systems drive the choice of executing the behavior or not. Coaches must help salespeople develop strong belief systems that will carry them through the behavioral roadblocks they may face in the course of their selling day.

The last performance measurement in the Success Triangle involves **technique,** or the actual selling skills necessary for success. Technique involves three areas: personal presence (the style the salesperson uses to build relationships and communicate), the salesperson's ability to ask the necessary questions to make the prospect or customer explore the potential of doing business, and the strategic use of the Sandler Selling System to close business.

THE 20/60/20 RULE

As I mentioned earlier, there are three categories of salespeople. Approximately 20% of all salespeople are categorized as high performers. Another 60% fall into the category of variable performer. The remaining 20% are categorized as low performers. I developed this 20/60/20 model as a coaching methodology arising out of the well-known Pareto principle, which holds that for many events, roughly 80% of the effects come from 20% of the causes. My assumption in this 20/60/20 Rule, borne out by direct experience with countless sales teams over the years, is that high performers typically make up 20% of the talent pool of a given sales team (and contribute 80% of the revenue that team produces).

The effective coach uses the same coaching methodology, but applies different tactics in order to achieve success with each of the three groups since each category requires a personalized touch when it comes to supporting constructive change.

Coaching the top 20% requires goal-directed thinking. The top 20% are typically motivated by recognition and goals that stretch their accomplishments. Even the problems faced by the top 20% can be turned into goals, rather than being viewed as roadblocks. Balance is key to working with these high performers, so the coach typically helps them work on three professional goals and two personal goals each day (the Rule of Three and Two mentioned earlier). The three professional goals are designed to help them be more effective in their sales role, and the two personal goals are designed to ensure that their belief in themselves strengthens as their professional goals are achieved. An example of a professional goal would be hitting a certain measurable prospecting target for a given day. An example of a personal goal would be improving an exercise regimen. Working out has a positive effect on the salesperson, and this good feeling carries over into the workplace. This powerful Rule of Three and Two prevents burnout and develops a pace for success.

Coaching the middle 60% requires goals that build traction over time. Small goals that build on the success of the previous goal develop a success track that, if continuously applied, will help the middle 60% move upward toward the top 20%. The goals must be small but not too easily accomplished. The coach must find the balance between challenging and overloading this group since too much pressure will cause procrastination and anxiety. Momentum and unceasing reinforcement are keys to helping this group succeed because it is easy for these salespeople to lose focus and fall back into old, non-productive habits.

Coaching the bottom 20% provides the greatest challenge of all. The coach working with salespeople in this group tests their willingness to change and grow. The focus of this group is typically excuse-making, so the coach usually works with them on the development of an unconditional commitment to success. Although it sounds harsh, the majority of the people in this bottom 20% should be managed out of the company. Why? Too many sales managers spend the majority of their time trying to help these salespeople perform at an acceptable level, usually without success. Salespeople in the bottom 20% typically have the aptitude to succeed, but lack the willingness to perform. The effective coach develops a plan and gains the personal buy-in to work through the four transition steps. Very often, those in this group stall out at stage one, denial, or stage two, resistance. They may be good at developing the plan, but they are likely to give only lip service to the execution. The same small goal process used with the 60% group is the key to helping this group grow; however, it's important to remember that the people in this group must prove, by their actions, that they really are worthy of the coach's time.

THE THREE C'S OF SUCCESS

With all of these groups, the effective coach learns to recognize, evaluate, and support the Three C's of Success: **conviction**, **commitment**, and **competency**. Here are three coaching questions that will help with the evaluation.

- *Do the salespeople have the **conviction** to continually challenge themselves to execute behavior in an ever-improving way—and do they consistently work on their belief system so it supports growth?* All high-performing salespeople focus on improving success on a daily basis. They recognize that growth occurs because they analyze better ways to execute their behavior and develop aspirational beliefs to support it.

- *Do the salespeople demonstrate unconditional **commitment** to success and a "do what it takes" attitude that gets them through the selling challenges they face?* All high-performing salespeople recognize that their commitment will be challenged on a daily basis. They find a way to build an internal system keeping their backbone strong when times are tough.

- *Do the salespeople have enough **competency** and proficiency with the Sandler Selling System to accomplish sales goals?* All high-performing salespeople are consistently improving selling effectiveness because they realize that they have to be one step ahead of today's buyer. There is no room for complacency. Technological and social shifts are likely to transform markets and shake up industries overnight; prospects today have more information, due to the Internet, than they have ever had in the past. As a result, a salesperson's "A" game of yesterday may no longer keep him ahead of the curve today.

There is an addendum to this list of questions, one that supports all three of the C's I have shared with you: *Do the salespeople approach their jobs with a "more, better, and different" attitude about any behavioral roadblocks confronting them?* High-performing salespeople approach their jobs with a "failure is not an option" attitude. They understand, in the face of a shortfall, they may have to do more of a behavior, adopt a better behavior, or execute a totally different behavior in order to succeed.

THIS IS NOT A SPRINT

Let me reinforce one vitally important point before we move on: This is a long-term game. Effective coaches understand that change takes time and requires a significant personal commitment on their part, as well as on the part of the salesperson. The coaching experience must be viewed as a marathon, not a sprint. Constructive, sustainable change cannot be rushed; the salesperson who pretends it can may help generate a false sense of security on the part of the coach, but won't develop the necessary behavior, attitude, and technique.

Measurable progress is the goal. Very often, such progress comes in small doses.

SANDLER COACHING RULES

- Encourage your salespeople to stretch their comfort zone in order to achieve greater success.
- Coach your salespeople through denial and resistance before exploring options for development.
- Model and teach salespeople how to internalize the four-step process for eliminating persistent negative thoughts.
- Use the Sandler Success Triangle as the cornerstone of coaching.
- Customize each coaching session according to the 20/60/20 Rule.

CHAPTER FOUR

Take the X-ray

OVERVIEW

- Goals drive coaching
- The "As is/To be" growth gap
- Understanding skills, knowledge, and application benchmarks
- The power of behavioral assessment

This chapter tells how to conduct a "sales X-ray" to determine what's really going on in the salesperson's world—and why. This is an essential prerequisite to effective goal-setting, which is a central element to coaching success. You will also learn why the salesperson and coach must work together to identify and pursue goals if they are to achieve success.

GOALS DRIVE COACHING

Salespeople typically fit into one of two discipline sets: **goal setters** or **problem solvers**. Goal setters design the success they are committed to achieving and grow in the direction of the goals they continuously pursue. Problem solvers follow a career of default, using the problems they solve as a catalyst for whatever growth they expect to experience in their professional life.

Study after study has shown that less than 20% of all salespeople are goal setters. This elite group generally outperforms and out-earns the other group. Let me clarify what that means: The income of the minority of salespeople who set goals is predictably and consistently greater than that of the 80-plus percent who don't—combined!

It's not that surprising that the income figures break down the way they do. Goal setting is difficult and requires unconditional commitment as well as a strategic mindset. To shift salespeople from one group to the other requires a coach who is willing to conduct a "sales X-ray" to determine what's going on in the salesperson's world—and why.

PETER'S STORY

Peter, a coaching client, has worked with me for the last five years. A man in his early 40s, Peter feels he's at the midpoint of his sales career. Many younger salespeople, Peter says, are beginning to eclipse him in the eyes of his sales manager. Peter feels that he is being stereotyped as a "steady Eddy" sales performer, someone who lacks the passion associated with higher achievement. Early in his career he was a top performer, and other salespeople wanted to be like him. He set the standard for success and was an icon in the sales department. By the time he started working with me, it seemed he had reached a plateau. He was concerned about his future with the company.

In our early coaching sessions, we analyzed the difference between Peter's early success and what he was experiencing now. Together, we determined that, at the beginning of his career, he had high ambition and a strong personal drive to do whatever it took to be the number one salesperson in the company. His initiative and vitality drove him to perform the kinds of daily behaviors that made others look at him in awe.

More recently, though, we found he was relying on his past successes more than his desire to create new success. He was no longer as invested in setting standards for new business development that would become the benchmarks for other salespeople on the team. Not only had he been coasting, he had gotten used to coasting. That depressed him.

Once we uncovered it, changing this current behavior pattern seemed like an insurmountable task to Peter. He had almost resigned himself to it as the "new normal." But we designed a series of coaching sessions driven by setting small professional goals. These were designed to inch Peter back up the success scale. Additionally, we created some personal goals to change Peter's internal attitude and help him feel better about himself. Peter began a health campaign that included eating right and exercising more. I hoped that the better he felt about himself, the more he would be able to work on his more challenging professional goals.

It worked. The personal goals worked in conjunction with the professional ones to rebuild Peter's confidence. Gradually, his newly acquired confidence yielded greater and greater levels of success. As Peter began to achieve the small goals, he reached to achieve even larger goals, widening the gap between himself and the rest of the sales team.

Peter's commitment to goals, both personal and professional, were the keys to unlocking his potential for success. Within two years of our first coaching meeting, Peter was once again the talk of the company—and the sales leader others set their sights to become.

THE VISION FACTOR

High-performing salespeople typically find a way to see the result of their selling efforts clearly—ahead of time. Vision is the starting point, followed by mission and strategy. These three areas must be determined prior to the salesperson beginning the goal-setting process. Otherwise, the coach will not be able to help the salesperson make progress toward accomplishing goals.

- **Vision:** a picture of success salespeople see in their minds. For instance: *To become the best salesperson in the industry.*

- **Mission:** the pre-established objective of the vision. For instance: *To master the Sandler strategies and tactics to better control the results of sales calls.*

- **Strategy:** a specific plan to accomplish the mission over a defined period of time. For instance: *To develop a behavior Cookbook for Success (see definition on next page) focusing on the top ten selling behaviors.*

These three lead to the:

- **Goal(s):** one or more ends to which effort is directed. The goal or goals identified should be such that the salesperson can accomplish specific, measurable key performance indicators that yield the results needed to succeed.

Goals give salespeople a sense of control of their business destiny—as well as power over life in general. This personal control is a strong motivating factor in high performers so it is important for the coach to fully understand the role goal setting will play in the coaching session. The effective coach knows that the salesperson and the coach need to work through the vision, mission, and strategy discussions before they attempt to identify the actual goal. That's what I did in concert with Peter, and what I recommend you do in the early stages of your interactions with any salesperson you are coaching.

? WHAT DOES IT MEAN?

Sandler's Cookbook for Success, created by and for the salesperson being coached, is essential to the sales coaching process. This is a list of measurable activities and behaviors that the salesperson commits to doing every day and every week, at certain predetermined numeric levels, in order to be successful. Note that this is not something that the manager imposes upon the salesperson; rather, it is a written document that the salesperson creates and consults daily in support of his own mission.

THE RULE OF THREE AND TWO, REVISITED

As we have seen, top salespeople work on the Sandler coaching Rule of Three and Two by focusing on three professional goals and two personal goals. The three professional goals are designed to keep the salesperson growing in the job, while the two personal goals are designed to bolster an inner sense of worth. This concept follows Sandler's Identity/Role Theory, which is (as I hope you've gathered by now) foundational to the coaching process and which carries an importance in all that we'll be discussing in the pages ahead. In Sandler terms, Identity and Role are the key elements of self-worth and are summed up in the Sandler principle, "You can only perform in your roles in a manner consistent with how you see yourself."

S.M.A.R.T. GOALS

The goal-setting process is an essential early phase of any successful coaching encounter. It requires an environmental scan analyzing the internal strengths and weaknesses of the salesperson. The effective coach fully understands salespeople's situations, works with them to identify and formalize relevant goals, and creates a success track to measure their accomplishment. This success track becomes a roadmap that all coaching sessions impact; it fuels the salesperson's passion for selling, beginning with anticipation and ending with achievement.

A critical early responsibility of the coach is to help the salesperson set realistic goals, using S.M.A.R.T. principles (specific, measurable, attainable, realistic, time bound) to assess goals, refine them, and develop an exact timeline for achieving them. The establishment of such goals is an anchor for all successful coaching sessions. It is non-negotiable because it develops mutual understanding between the coach and salesperson and creates a shared commitment to the outcome.

GROWTH GAPS

The growth gap is the space between the current accomplishment level of the salesperson and the desired future level of accomplishment. In other words, the growth gap contrasts how the salesperson is performing defined selling behaviors at this moment in time with the level of performance committed to developing by a specific future time.

Here's why a discussion of growth gaps is important. The effective coach focuses the conversation on the behavior, characteristics, attributes, and competency performance levels the salesperson is committed to developing by a predetermined date in the future. The salesperson must take a realistic snapshot of today's performance as a starting point and determine realistic growth over a defined period of time. For example, a salesperson who is struggling with consistently prospecting for new business may rate himself a 3 on a scale of 1 to 10. Let's assume the coach agrees with that assessment. The salesperson's goal may be to become a 5 over the next six months. The growth gap would be 2, and the coach's job would be to determine the behavior the salesperson must perform over the next six months to earn a rating of 5. This kind of discussion forces the salesperson to reflect on how he currently sees his Role performance and creates a meaningful personal commitment to measured improvement over time.

Such a process—which I call an "As is/To be" analysis—involves documenting specific behaviors, attributes, and skills in order to define the current capabilities of the salesperson as a way of benchmarking the present performance. There is no other effective way to establish future performance targets.

Ideally, both the salesperson and coach come to a point of agreement on where the salesperson should invest time and resources for growth. Together, they can create a prioritized roadmap for success. This gap analysis requires enough detail for the salesperson to see clearly both the impact of current behavior and the need for new, higher-performing behavior.

To effectively carry out the gap analysis, it is important to identify the salesperson's specific objectives and goals for future performance, and then to gather the necessary information on current performance in order to build clear, exacting, and mutually agreed-upon steps for growth.

SKILLS, KNOWLEDGE, AND APPLICATION

Three major problems may present obstacles to the attainment of goals, and the coach must be aware of their potential impact before each coaching session.

The selling **skills** necessary for success in the sales position must be clearly defined. Once the current level of skill in each relevant area is established, the next area for focus is the salesperson's **knowledge** of what to do with those skills in the context of the job. The last area of attention for the coach is to determine whether or not there is consistent **application** of the skills and knowledge when the salesperson is in the line of fire. The coaching process will fail if the manager assumes the salesperson's level of expertise is higher than it actually is.

Let's take a moment to look at each of these areas in greater depth.

Skills

An understanding of the current skill set is the starting point for coaching success; however, focusing too much on skill tends to turn coaching into training. The coach's job is to understand whether or not the salesperson has the top ten behaviors necessary for success. If the coach determines the skills do not exist or they are weak, the salesperson must be sent to training to further develop the skills prior to coaching.

Here is a list you've seen before. It reflects the top ten behaviors salespeople should be able to execute in the context of an outside sales position.

1. **Lead generation:** Prospecting, the number one behavior that drives all the others.

2. **Building relationships:** Establishing a strong, open relationship based on trust.

3. **Qualifying opportunity:** Determining a reason to do business.

4. **Making presentations:** Presenting solutions to the prospect's problems.

5. **Servicing customers:** Delivering superior customer satisfaction.

6. **Account management:** Maximizing business in each account.

7. **Territory development:** Building a strategy to grow the territory.

8. **Building a Cookbook for Success:** Establishing productive sales activity.

9. **Continuous education:** Developing ongoing product, market, and sales knowledge.

10. **Execution of the Sandler Selling System:** Mastering the sales process.

As you know, the coach must be able to rate the salesperson's ability to execute each of these ten skill sets on the scale of 1 to 10 as a way to determine whether training or coaching is necessary to resolve the issues the salesperson is facing. If the rating for any skill is below 7, training on that skill set to improve execution may be necessary before coaching can be effective. If the skill is in the 7 to 10 range, the coach must analyze the salesperson's knowledge of when to utilize the skill, since many salespeople have skills but are unaware of the situations in which the skill is applicable.

I emphasize these points for a reason. "As is/To be" analysis will always be an important part of skill growth, regardless of the level of success the salesperson attains. No matter how well someone performs a selling skill, there is always room for growth and improvement.

Coaching salespeople to increase their skill level is a key area of focus for the coach. The coach's job is to focus the salesperson on three important concepts to personally drive growth. The key words here, as you may recall, are: more, better, or different. In order to improve skills, the salesperson may have to do more of a specific behavior to gain success. In other cases, the salesperson may have to find better ways to execute the behavior. Lastly, the salesperson may have to focus on a totally different way of executing the skill to be more effective.

There will always be targets for skill improvement in each of the ten categories I've shared with you. If you doubt that, ask yourself: How important was a working knowledge of LinkedIn to the salespeople who were prospecting in 2001? How important is such expertise today?

These three words—more, better, and different—help salespeople understand the way improving a skill set is within their power and a driver of selling success. Viewing growth this way helps counteract the "plateau effect" many salespeople experience, in which an ability to execute behavior is held hostage by an outdated skill set.

Knowledge

Knowledge, for salespeople, is based in the understanding of when and how a given skill is to be used during the sales process.

Many salespeople have the skill set necessary for success. However, they struggle with knowing exactly when and how to use the skill in a given situation. It's easy for an unskilled coach to be fooled into thinking that a salesperson who "has all the skills" is guaranteed success. The effective coach helps the salesperson role-play the execution of the skill during the coaching session in order to determine whether or not the salesperson has the ability to apply it in context.

During the role-play session, salespeople must explain their understanding of the situation, review the specific skill they have chosen to apply, and describe the outcome they are committed to achieving. This "real world" role-play allows the coach to review the flow of the sales call and determine the cause of the salespeople's problems.

Rick's Story

Rick, a 10-year sales veteran, was having major issues with creating rapport during his sales calls. He felt that he was properly executing the first two compartments of the Sandler Submarine, Bonding & Rapport and Up-Front Contracts, but reported that his prospects were "aloof" and "detached." When I quizzed him about the strategy he was employing to strengthen the relationship with his prospects, he clearly explained the science of neuro-linguistic programming (NLP), primary sensory dominance, and the elements of a strong up-front contract. During the coaching session role-play, I determined that Rick was inadvertently using tonal qualities that made his prospect feel very "not-OK."

Rick's vocal tones were sharp and dominating when he made his points. He was coming across as aggressive, which was shutting down his prospects. I advised him to lower his tonality one half octave below his normal speaking voice and to act a little not-OK at the beginning of his sales call.

He did. The results were extraordinary. As Rick struggled on purpose in front of his prospects, they opened up and began to rescue him—instead of building their defenses and fighting him.

The role-play helped us determine he was using the Sandler skills taught in the Bonding & Rapport class literally—as it was laid out on the page—without implementing the subtle nuances necessary to soften his approach. Coaching helped Rick determine the delicate balance that he needed to establish in order to be more successful. Knowing the right answers was not enough.

Many salespeople apply Sandler strategies and tactics "right out of the box" without personalizing them to the specific selling situation. Rick was one of them, and the effective coach can expect to run into many more.

Application

Practice, as the saying goes, makes perfect. Application is the key to salespeople sustaining success; it's the process of turning learned skills into consistent, repeatable behaviors. High-performing salespeople understand the link between behavior and success. These sales winners continually apply the proper behavior associated with success, even though they may struggle occasionally when it comes to achieving the desired result.

The top ten behaviors I reviewed earlier are only effective if they are regularly utilized during the sales process. The high-performing salesperson turns these skills into application goals. For example, for field salespeople, prospecting has five associated Sandler subset skills: cold calling, correspondence, networking, referrals, and business introductions. Each of these subset skills must have a weekly execution goal associated with them. A salesperson might commit to making twenty-five cold calls per day, sending out ten prospecting emails per day, going to one networking event per week, giving one referral to a client per week, and scheduling one business introduction lunch per week as part of a business-building plan. The consistent application of these prospecting behaviors, measured against the weekly performance goal, allows the salesperson to achieve greater success. The effective coach analyzes this application factor to determine the correct coaching strategy to help the salesperson improve.

I would estimate that about 60% of salespeople fail because they utilize their skills only sporadically—and another 20% fail because they are unwilling to execute the skill in question due to existing beliefs and behavior patterns that don't support high achievement. The effective coach helps the 60% group set modest application goals to gain traction and then conducts regular coaching sessions to spur consistent growth. As harsh as this sounds, the coach should not spend any time with a salesperson in the bottom 20% group once it's determined that the person has chosen not to apply skills due to discomfort. Unwillingness to change old habits is, frankly, an insurmountable barrier. If you are certain a person has no intention to grow and is wasting valuable coaching resources, it is, in all likelihood, time to part ways.

THE POWER OF THE BEHAVIORAL ASSESSMENT

Up to this point in the book, you've probably noticed that I've emphasized observation and interaction. The coach observes the salespeople performing their jobs and interacts with them in a coaching session to bring about the necessary behavioral modifications. Although

SANDLER COACHING INSIGHT

Ongoing coaching develops accountability in the salesperson and ensures the ongoing execution of the skills necessary for consistent success. David Sandler used to say: "Do the behaviors! Do the behaviors! Do the behaviors!" Once you have worked with a salesperson to identify the vision, mission, strategy, and goals, your job is, at the end of the day, to make sure you send the same basic message in a supportive, positive way.

observation and interaction are important, it's equally important to be able to look inside the salesperson, as it were, and identify the "hardwired" issues that are either driving success or preventing it.

This is accomplished with an internal behavioral assessment designed to create a neutral, unvarnished view of key competencies and behaviors particular to each individual salesperson. These assessments analyze internal views, biases, choices, motivations, characteristics, and attitudes about specific selling behaviors within the salesperson and develop a profile that benchmarks these against the actions of successful salespeople. All salespeople who take the evaluation are measured against these behavioral benchmarks.

There are two evaluations currently used by Sandler franchisees: one is provided by The Devine Group and the other by Extended DISC. Each has standalone merit and provides critical information to help anyone from the CEO of a company to members of the sales team grow in ways they might not normally expect. These invaluable tools can be customized and shaped to yield critical information the coach can utilize to help the individual salesperson eliminate common pitfalls preventing superior performance.

❓ WHAT DOES IT MEAN?

The Devine Inventory™ is a battery of assessments that allow employers to focus on a wide range of skills and behaviors and evaluate how those skills and behaviors are likely to affect workplace performance.

DISC evaluations are behavior assessment tools based on the DISC theory of psychologist William Moulton Marston, which centers on four different behavioral traits: Dominant, Influencer, Steady Relator, and Compliant.

For more information about the Devine Inventory and DISC evaluations, visit www.sandler.com/online-training/training-assessment.

THE DEVINE GROUP

Headquartered in Cincinnati, Ohio, The Devine Group has been a leader in assessments for more than forty years. Established in 1970, the company has helped thousands of clients strengthen their organizations through talent management tools. The Devine Group provides clients with human resource tools spanning the employee lifecycle, including talent acquisition, development planning, and performance management.

By analyzing the behavioral tendencies of individual

salespeople, coaches can assess traits such as: work ethic, specific selling behaviors and attitudes, commitment to success, and so on. One of the reasons the Devine Inventory assessment was created is to help coaches build a knowledgeable, responsive, high-performing culture within the sales team.

MICHELLE'S STORY

Michelle is a salesperson who has had an up-and-down sales career. Her sales manager Caleb was becoming more and more frustrated with Michelle's inability to sustain consistent progress. Caleb understood the importance of coaching as a way to help Michelle grow, but somehow couldn't break through to the real issue that was holding Michelle back.

Michelle took the Devine Inventory. When I analyzed it, I found some startling information. I told Caleb: "Michelle's sales motor is broken!"

There are five key behaviors embedded in the sales motor: goal setting, initiative, vitality, ego, and time management. The Devine Inventory assessment determined that Michelle was a problem solver, not a goal setter—which meant she was easily distracted during the course of her day. Additionally, Michelle's vitality score was extremely low. Usually, she was running out of energy at the day's midpoint. Lastly, Michelle's ego score was very high, which prevented her from looking inward to gain personal insight and confidence.

I helped Caleb work with Michelle to set some goals and create a sense of balance in Michelle's life. Next Caleb recommended an exercise regimen to help Michelle maintain the vital energy that she needed throughout her day. Thanks to these simple changes, Michelle's performance improved.

Without the behavioral assessment, Caleb never would have determined the internal issues Michelle was facing.

EXTENDED DISC

Extended DISC, a company located in Woodlands, Texas, was created over twenty years ago with a vision of providing clients the information they need to become more successful. Offering a suite of scientifically validated, online tools used by thousands of organizations all over the world, the Extended DISC assessment helps clients develop a confident self-awareness that enables decisions about how to modify behaviors to improve the ability to interact with others.

Specifically, Extended DISC provides salespeople with a map to more successful interactions with others by showing them how to modify their behavior to better communicate, motivate, influence, and lead.

TOM'S STORY

Tom is a strong personality who needs to be in control of every selling situation. He used the Sandler sales process as though it were a weapon strapped to his belt to crush prospects who tried to put their needs over his.

His up-front contracts aggressively developed the expectations for sales calls and were always designed to deliver the narrowly defined outcome he needed to occur. (Incidentally, this defeats the purpose of such a contract.) Tom's questions for uncovering pain were perfectly executed—and he always seemed to celebrate the ensuing pain he uncovered.

In Tom's mind, he was flawlessly executing the Sandler system. He couldn't understand why his closing rate was embarrassingly low.

I had Tom take the Extended DISC profile. He was astonished at its lessons: His ability to understand and react to the prospect's communication style was abysmally low.

Extended DISC categorized Tom as someone who would be tempted to conduct himself in such a way to always gain control of any selling situation regardless of the needs of his prospect. Many of the people in Tom's category become superb communicators and expert practitioners of the Sandler Selling System. The problem was, Tom was not yet one of them. He was steamrolling his prospects.

During our coaching sessions, Tom learned new ways to modify his behavior and tailor the Sandler sales process to meet the needs of his prospects instead of his own. Tom began to work steadfastly on his communication issues. The impact was immediate and positive. The Sandler strategies and tactics worked better than they ever had once Tom developed a deeper awareness of the environment he had to create to open the minds of his various prospects. The questions in the Extended DISC evaluation gave him insight into the problems he was inadvertently causing and helped him react to the needs of his prospects rather than manipulate the prospect into a no-win corner.

Both the Devine Inventory and Extended DISC give coaches the insight to raise awareness of the internal blockages preventing salespeople from achieving their true potential. They should be considered core components of the "sales X-ray."

SANDLER COACHING RULES

- Encourage your salespeople to unconditionally commit to setting personal and professional goals as a key part of the coaching process.

- Develop the top ten behaviors for each salesperson and encourage salespeople to measure themselves with a mix of behaviors and numbers instead of only numbers.

- Use the "As is/To be" growth gap to benchmark the current level of skill, and set time-bound goals to improve the application of each skill.

- Use behavioral assessments to analyze the internal strengths and weaknesses driving or inhibiting success.

- Invest coaching time into salespeople who are unconditionally committed to success, not the bottom 20% who give "lip service" to it.

CHAPTER FIVE

Building Trust and Comfort

OVERVIEW

- The coaching contract, revisited
- An environment of trust
- Well/better partnership
- Head trash and baggage removal
- Neuro-linguistic programming
- Transactional analysis

This chapter covers the importance of setting ground rules for the coaching engagement to create an environment of trust and comfort for both the coach and the salesperson. Additionally, it will review the psychological factors influencing the success of coaching sessions.

THE COACHING CONTRACT, REVISITED

I've already briefly discussed the up-front contract. It's time now to look at it more closely to see how it can be used to establish a more formal coaching contract.

Without trust, effective sales coaching is impossible; without a good coaching contract, trust between salesperson and coach is all but impossible to achieve. That's why it is so important to establish an agreement or verbal contract for the coaching process, much like the Sandler up-front contract salespeople use to set expectations and ensure a mutually beneficial outcome for sales calls. Like the up-front contract, the coaching contract covers the rules of engagement and creates a roadmap to follow during the sessions.

There are six critical elements of the coaching contract: the goals for the coaching session; the time commitment for the session; the agenda that details the exact topics to be covered; the coaching methodology to be utilized; the environment to be created; and lastly, the follow-up actions to stay on track.

1. **Goals:** Whoever initiates the session is in charge of establishing the goals. Goals must be crystal clear. Some typical goals for the coaching session are: analyzing specific

problems, correcting behavioral issues, understanding internal problems the salesperson might be facing, etc.

2. **Time:** The intended duration of the session itself as well as follow-up time commitments must be set and honored. If the coaching sessions are ongoing, each session must have its own specific coaching contract to outline the specific time commitment for that day. A one-hour coaching session has three components: ten minutes to set the agenda and review past action steps, forty minutes to delve into the new agenda item, and ten minutes to anchor learning and establish new action steps.

3. **Agenda:** There must be a clear, realistic agenda for the coaching session that assesses the issues from the salesperson's as well as coach's perspective. Once the agenda is established, the time commitment must be analyzed carefully by both sides to ensure there is enough time set aside to deal with the issues.

4. **Methodology:** The coach must outline the specific steps in the Sandler Coaching System (as outlined in Chapter Six of this book) to make sure the salesperson understands each step. Specifically, the coach must outline the step or steps that are the focus of that day's session. The coach must also make sure that the salesperson is comfortable with the entire agenda.

5. **Environment:** The coaching environment must be open and honest so both parties can communicate openly. The

physical and mental environment must be comfortable so it supports candid conversation. The physical environment should be private and free of interruptions. The mental environment must be free of doubt and uncertainty; everything between the coach and salesperson must be transparent.

6. **Actions:** These can be as simple as the exploration of a new way the salesperson will behave or think, or as complex as a behavior modification program taking multiple sessions to achieve. But the session must be focused on doing, not on talking or making excuses.

SUPPORTING AN ENVIRONMENT OF TRUST

Trust is a particularly important factor. Let's look at it in depth.

All effective coaches understand the importance of developing trust and the significant role trust plays in coaching success. The salesperson and coach must learn to trust each other as well as the coaching process if their work together is to succeed, and this only comes about as a result of each party identifying a way to gain and sustain the other's trust. The Sandler-trained coach focuses on the Three P's of Trust in order to foster this atmosphere: **potency, permission,** and **protection.** Each must be present in the coaching contract to create the proper environment. These three elements are so important that they are worth a detailed look.

Potency

All corporate hierarchy roles should be put aside during the coaching process. These roles imply a power relationship over a subordinate and will inhibit the openness necessary to deal with more deeply imbedded issues the salesperson is facing. It is important to approach the coaching process from a level perspective—peer-to-peer. Taking potency out of play is the first step in developing an open atmosphere in which the salesperson can share the meaningful information necessary for the coach to know if the two of them are dealing with the real issues. I have often advised sales managers to ask this question: "Is it all right for me to take my sales manager hat off for this session and ask you some difficult questions so I can fully understand the entire issue?"

Permission

The coach must grant salespeople permission to speak freely and to share unguarded information without fear of judgment. If the salesperson withholds critical information or only shares it cautiously or unwillingly, coaching may fail because the coach will be dealing with non-threatening surface issues instead of real problems. In early coaching sessions, many salespeople hide behind a protective wall of evasion, unwilling to share feelings, shortcomings, failures, and similar topics. Speaking freely in front of a superior may have caused problems in the past. If the environment is comfortable and trust-based, sharing personal thoughts, feelings of vulnerability, awkward moments, and fear of failure will help the coach get to the root of the problem and deal with the real issues. Permission to speak freely is a key concept in the coaching contract, and it has to be established on the front end of each coaching session.

Protection

In order to help salespeople to feel comfortable speaking freely, the coach must assure them that they are protected from future reprisal for anything said during the coaching process. This is critical in building a trusting environment and will help the coaching session be conducted with total candor instead of restrained conversation. The coaching session will be ineffective if the salesperson feels there's a possibility for a "gotcha" that will result in punishment. The exception to protection, of which both parties must be aware, comes when the salesperson admits to unethical or illegal behavior. This behavior does not fall under the protection umbrella and should be handled separately, with the salesperson being aware of the consequences.

THE WELL/BETTER PARTNERSHIP

The coach is charged with creating an environment that salespeople feel is focused on helping them become a better version of themselves—not simply more effective in the sales role.

The easiest way to accomplish this is to focus on creating a "well/better partnership," in which each session begins with the coach expressing appreciation for a behavior, attitude, or technique the salesperson has performed well that is associated with issues being covered that day. Many coaches begin their coaching sessions in earnest with the question, "What are three things you believe you did well during your last sales call?" This building block creates a positive start to the coaching session, and it reflects the reality that every sales call has elements, as small as they may be, that the salesperson performed well.

Beginning with an affirmative thought sets the stage for a positive coaching session. Without this question, many salespeople view coaching as a punitive process, something that erodes their identity over time.

SELF-WORTH

David Sandler incorporated his theory on self-worth in the Sandler sales methodology as a way to help salespeople understand the importance of belief in self. Understanding the various ways to influence the self-worth of a salesperson is an integral component of sales success, as well as coaching success. Effective sales coaches build trust by positively influencing the salesperson's self-worth.

Let me remind you once again that David Sandler believed that self-worth, for salespeople and everyone else, is made up of two separate components: Identity (who we are intrinsically) and Role (the behavior we perform in the various areas of our personal and professional life). Sandler proposed that each component should have a measurement scale of 1 to 10 associated with it to identify its strength. He also insisted that both components should be kept separate from one another in order for individuals to improve and grow as people. Although this principle holds true in all situations for all people, I mention it again because it's particularly relevant to the salesperson, who is quite likely to face performance challenges arising from having mixed the two components up.

Traditionally, salespeople are taught to improve their success by focusing on the development of their Role performance. Sandler argued that this was not enough.

JILL'S STORY

Jill, a Sandler client, was struggling with cold calling. She arranged a coaching session with me to specifically work on the issue. Jill was extremely frustrated by the time we met. She told me she made 369 cold calls over the previous three weeks with zero success.

When I asked how she was trying to change that situation, she said in a very forceful, frustrated way, "That's why I'm here! I don't know what I'm doing wrong. Maybe I'm just bad at cold calling."

That seemed unlikely. A year or so prior, Jill had been a stellar cold caller. Something had changed.

Most recently, she had committed to making 250 cold calls on a new product line in a three-week period. When she didn't have any success, her manager told her to "just make more calls." But with each additional call Jill spiraled deeper into feelings of failure and self-doubt. Her Role failure, as a cold caller, translated into Identity failure. She continuously beat herself up with self-deprecating rants. Jill's Identity and Role had become muddled into one.

The first step was to detach the two components and work on each separately. Prior to these cold-calling struggles, Jill had a strong belief in herself and was confidently experiencing a great deal of success as a cold caller. The first step in our coaching process was to build two growth tracks, one focusing on her inner confidence and the other focused on her outer performance. In other words, we improved her inner belief in herself—Identity performance—so she could clearly develop more effective cold-calling behavior—Role performance.

As Jill made cold calls, she agreed to work on the first track by improving the quality of her personal life. Jill resumed an exercise regimen, going to the health club each morning at 5:00 A.M. as she used to do when she was experiencing success. She also began reading biographical novels again, something that had always made her happy. She joined a book club to surround herself with like-minded people. Lastly, she instituted "date night" with her husband once a week.

A remarkable transformation took place. As the weeks passed, Jill began to experience the cold-calling success she once had on the phone. As her belief in herself returned, her former confident self emerged. This allowed her to clearly examine the specific Sandler phone skills she was executing and better deliver her message to the prospects on the other end of the phone. Jill

SANDLER COACHING INSIGHT

Trust in self is a powerful driver of success. When a salesperson loses this personal trust, it is difficult to institute the changes necessary for growth. The coach must help the salesperson understand the importance of nurturing Identity as the salesperson deals with the separate challenge of improving Role performance. This requires the removal of "head trash."

? WHAT DOES IT MEAN?

Head trash is an accumulation of beliefs, attitudes, biases, untested thoughts, and general misinformation collected by the subconscious mind over a period of years. If these inner thoughts are allowed to grow and are not eliminated, they create baggage carried throughout life preventing greater personal and professional success.

How many salespeople make judgments like, "It's useless to cold call on a Monday morning because no one answers their phone"? Or "Friday afternoons are not productive because prospects are busy wrapping up the week"? These false beliefs may shorten the workweek to four days and rob the unsuspecting salesperson of 20% of his weekly productivity.

Head trash is often blindly accepted and followed, creating judgments about the actions a salesperson should take or the direction he should follow in business as well as life. Unfortunately, following this path negatively impacts the potential for success and creates the missed opportunities that separate high performers from mediocre ones.

learned she hadn't lost her skills; she had allowed Role failure to drive Identity failure.

After three weekly coaching sessions, she had rebuilt the internal support system necessary for greater success.

TAKING OUT THE HEAD TRASH, UNPACKING THE BAGGAGE

The coach must understand the root cause, or core belief, creating the head trash since it must be conquered at the innermost level. Visualize an archery target having three rings: the outer ring is labeled with the word "rules," the middle ring is labeled with the word "guidelines," and the inner ring is labeled with the word "core beliefs."

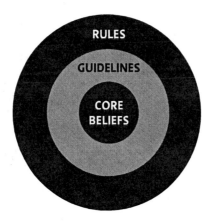

In order to identify and get rid of head trash, the coach must work with the inner ring, the core beliefs, of the salesperson rather than trying to change the salesperson's outer ring, or "rules." Let me share a story that will illustrate what I mean.

STEPHANIE'S STORY

I have a client, Stephanie, who came to me believing she could not close business in the professional services business sector. Each time she received a lead and made a follow-up sales call on a prospect in this world, her subconscious mind began to put negative thoughts in her head.

This was a problem because about 40% of Stephanie's prospect base is in this business segment. Her anxiety rose every time she had to make a sales call. When Stephanie first came to me for help, she asked me to teach her how to be more successful. I quickly realized it had nothing to do with her skills and everything to do with her head trash. We began to examine her beliefs and found she felt inadequate operating in a more professional world than the one in which she began her career. She certainly had the talent, skills, and presence to be successful. However, she was sabotaging herself each time she found herself in this situation.

I worked with Stephanie's core beliefs. Eventually I helped her change them to create new guidelines so she felt more comfortable and was better able to use her talent whenever she found herself in the professional services world.

Stephanie's core belief was centered on her assumption that she didn't have the education she considered necessary to work in the world of professional services. That belief created the guideline of inadequacy and made her anxious on each sales call, preventing her from building a relationship of trust with her prospects.

A limiting rule had been created in Stephanie's mind. It sounded like this: "You can't close prospects in the world of professional services." She had tried unsuccessfully to change this rule many times. Together, we established a new, more productive rule: "I am a sales professional with the skill to help all clients achieve their goals."

When Stephanie began to see selling as a profession and began to view herself as professional, equal status was created and she became more comfortable. She now calls on prospects in this sector with no problem.

BAGGER VANCE, SALES COACH

Many years ago I saw the movie *The Legend of Bagger Vance*. It's the story of a (fictional) golf caddy who helps a golfer overcome the trauma of World War I. The movie has a good message as it explores the baggage, or psychological head trash, this golfer had to overcome in order to return to the past success that he had experienced on the golf course. My favorite quote from the movie is when the caddy, Bagger Vance, helps the golfer understand the importance of moving on in life: "The war is over. It's time to put the baggage down and keep walking."

That's not just great advice for golfers. It's great advice for sales-people, too. Far too many carry personal baggage throughout their career and never achieve the success they deserve. It is vitally important for the coach to understand the impact of head trash and baggage on the subconscious mind and create a relationship deep enough in trust to deal with them before they accumulate and cause deeper issues.

NEURO-LINGUISTIC PROGRAMMING

Drs. Richard Bandler and John Grinder developed the science of neuro-linguistic programming back in the 1970s, based on their understanding of the connection between neural processes, language, and behavioral patterns learned through observation. Effective sales coaches can develop a similar understanding. Neuro-linguistic programming allows salespeople to create new ways of interpreting both verbal and nonverbal communication.

Specifically, the coach can better understand the unspoken thoughts of salespeople by dialing into their body movements and vocal patterns. This heightened sensory acuity helps the coach understand the underlying messages being sent by salespeople during coaching sessions.

The effective sales coach must be keenly aware of the messages sent by the salesperson both verbally and nonverbally. Responding appropriately to these messages deepens and enhances trust in the relationship.

These messages present themselves in three very different forms: words, tonality, and body language. Of course, the coach and salesperson use words to communicate. However, if coaches focus on the words only, they may miss the true message being delivered. The actual words only account for a small fraction of communication. The coach must hear the words, process them, and then observe the style the salesperson uses to deliver them. It is critical to read the body language and hear the tonality as they either support the message or give the coach reason to doubt the message.

SANDLER COACHING INSIGHT

The total message you send to a salesperson includes not only the words you speak, but also your tone of voice and your body language. It is important that the message sent by one component is congruent with the messages sent by the other two. Incongruent or "mixed" messages will hinder your rapport-building efforts and jeopardize the trust you may have established. It's equally important to communicate using nonjudgmental language and remain emotionally neutral, especially if the underlying tone of a salesperson's message becomes hostile or judgmental.

As the coaching session moves forward, it is critical that the coach pay attention to the various ways body language and tonality confirm the message being delivered verbally—or undermine it. If the message by the salesperson is delivered in a congruent way, that is with words, tonality, and body language aligned, it's probably true (or at least perceived by the salesperson as true). However, if body language or tonality is misaligned with the message, the coach must probe deeper for the hidden meaning behind the words. A salesperson who suddenly begins to fidget when delivering the message is displaying discomfort, and the coach should dig deeper into what is being said. Similarly, when someone sitting in a comfortable position suddenly sits more upright, that person is sending a message that should be questioned. In both cases, the salesperson may be using truthful words and phrases, but the body language is saying, "I have hidden feelings about this subject." These kinds of micro-messages are imbedded in most conversations and must be explored to determine the overall reality of what is being said. (As an aside, this is how skilled poker players learn to pick up the subtle "tells" of their opponent, giving them a significant advantage during the game.)

I refer to this process as "looking for leakage." Leakage occurs when the subconscious mind is uncomfortable with the words that a person is saying, causing subtle awkward movements or changes in pitch, pace, facial expression, and loudness. These aspects can be recognized with practice, and the most effective coaches are quite good at recognizing them. Often salespeople will feel that the coach is reading their minds when digging deeper into superficial answers, not realizing the hidden messages they themselves are sending. When done properly and in a supportive environment, this kind of questioning deepens the bond of trust between coach and salesperson.

TRANSACTIONAL ANALYSIS

In the 1950s Dr. Eric Berne began to develop his theories of transactional analysis, the renowned "Parent, Adult, Child" theory. Berne believed the human brain acts like a recording device and stores experiences deep inside, along with the feelings associated with them. All communication between human beings is, in Berne's view, considered to be a "transaction"—an interaction where ideas, thoughts, and concepts, as well as feelings and emotions, are, to use his phrase, "bought and sold."

In transactional analysis, the Parent recording, or ego state, is the voice of authority, the Child recording represents emotions and feelings, and the Adult recording helps people make choices to determine the way they should act. The Parent recording is divided in half, with both Nurturing and Critical elements. Something like 70% of effective coaching is delivered through the Nurturing Parent recording, which is likely to provide comfort, be fully present, pose relevant questions, and gently suggest challenges that can lead to growth. The effective coach understands there is no place in the coaching environment for the Critical Parent, which is harsher and more inclined to find fault. By asking questions and giving directions in a nurturing way, the coach is able to create an environment where the salesperson is comfortable being vulnerable and sharing information freely.

The other 30% of effective coaching is delivered using the non-judgmental Adult recording. The questions and statements made by the coach using this recording are straightforward, morally neutral, fact-based, and nonthreatening. Use of this recording allows the coach to focus on behavior and actions as well as results without making judgments about the character of the salesperson. The effective coach never uses the want- and need-driven

Child recording to deliver coaching messages since such messages tend to be emotional in nature and ineffective. The coach must leave the Child recording at home and not bring any of the Child's powerful emotions into the coaching session as these invariably reduce the success of the interaction.

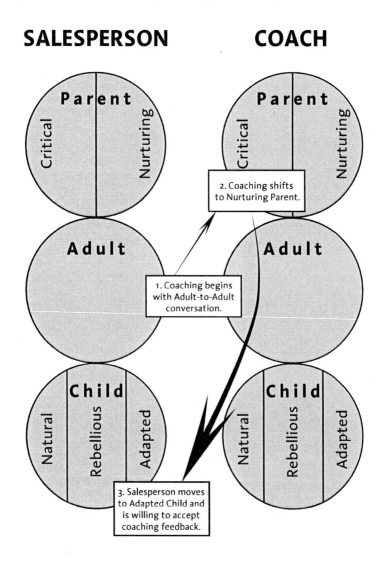

SALESPERSON   COACH

2. Coaching shifts to Nurturing Parent.

1. Coaching begins with Adult-to-Adult conversation.

3. Salesperson moves to Adapted Child and is willing to accept coaching feedback.

Transactional analysis helps the coach understand an important dynamic when communicating with a salesperson during a coaching session. The creation of a nurturing, nonjudgmental environment develops a "safe zone" of deep mutual trust that enables both parties to have candid conversations that result in improved performance by the salesperson.

I've spent an entire chapter elaborating on the various ways an effective coach builds and deepens a sense of trust and comfort with a salesperson, and I've done that at the risk of repeating some of the essential Sandler concepts I shared with you earlier in this book. This is for two reasons: first, because the Sandler concepts warrant repetition and reinforcement, even in printed form, and second, because the seven-step system I'll be sharing with you in the next chapter—the heart of the book—is useless without the ability to establish that trust and comfort. Please take the time to review all the concepts I've shared with you in this chapter one more time. Once you feel you are familiar with them, you will be ready to start examining the specifics of the Sandler Coaching System.

SANDLER COACHING RULES

- Set a strong coaching contract as a roadmap for success.
- Protect the Identity of the salesperson during the critique of the salesperson's Role.
- Help salespeople deal with the self-limiting beliefs robbing them of success.

- Make sure words align with body language and tonality during the coaching session.
- Stay in the Nurturing Parent and nonjudgmental Adult ego states during the session.

CHAPTER SIX

Coaching: A Process, Not an Event

OVERVIEW

- Experience and environment
- Strategic and tactical coaching
- The Sandler Coaching System
- A continuous coaching loop

This chapter will explore the importance of establishing a coaching process and viewing it as an ongoing development tool for the sales team. Effective coaching is not performed as a "one and done" model; rather, it is a tool for continuous improvement.

EXPERIENCE AND ENVIRONMENT

A good coaching session is part of an ongoing process. It's not a single event to be marked as "complete" on a checklist. The coach is responsible for creating a positive coaching experience, establishing a comfortable environment, bringing the expertise necessary to make the sessions effective, and following a clear plan. All of this takes thought, preparation, and methodology if the coaching is to be successful. Many coaches fail because they develop a "wing it" mentality—meaning they have no process at all. They treat the coaching process far too casually, and in so doing, they miss the opportunity to coach.

LUIS'S STORY

Luis is a successful sales manager. He prides himself on his understanding of his people, and his insights on their performance patterns have helped him achieve a great deal of success in guiding his salespeople to achieve company goals.

Yet Luis has a lot on his plate. His calendar is always jammed with the typical administrative and interpersonal duties a sales manager has to perform in the course of a week. Lately, as his staff has grown, he's felt more and more overbooked. Luis asked me for help. He wanted the team to perform even better.

I observed Luis interacting with his salespeople for a day and understood his problem. Luis is a new breed of manager. He leads a team of fifty Millennial inside-salespeople who sell over the phone. Each day he patrols the sales floor observing his people on the phone. From time to time, he stops to give someone advice when he hears a problem.

His typical "coaching session" was ten minutes long, and it was held on the sales floor so that there was no privacy. It consisted of Luis reviewing something he heard a salesperson say to a prospective customer that could have been handled better and explaining the various ways the salesperson could improve.

When Luis returned to his desk, there was a steady stream of salespeople entering and exiting his office all day long—each of them looking for his guidance to solve assorted additional sales issues. I noticed that many of the same problems showed up again and again. At the end of the day, Luis had solved all their issues—but he had spent no time leading the team toward higher performance.

In our coaching session, I helped Luis understand the role a formal coaching process might play in helping his people solve their own problems, instead of sapping his own time and energy by asking him to deal with the same issues over and over. Over the next two months, Luis's "coach on the fly" process evolved into a more formal coaching methodology. His salespeople began to use existing skills to resolve prospect and customer issues, to solve many more problems on their own, and to give him more time to truly lead the sales team.

EXPERIENCE

Luis was not coaching when I first started working with him, although that's what he thought he was doing. He was expeditiously solving problems and fixing issues as they arose so the department could keep running. Unfortunately, Luis was also creating "learned helplessness" by building an atmosphere where his people weren't growing. They had learned, over time, that it was easier to come to him to solve all their problems. This was Luis's decision; he was all too willing to put out the fires.

When I asked him why he acted this way, Luis responded with an emphatic, "That's my job!" I asked Luis what would change if for some reason he couldn't give his people the answers they wanted to day-to-day problems. He thought for a moment and said, "I guess they would have to figure it out on their own."

Then I asked if there were a benefit to Luis's team getting the answers for themselves. After a second, he responded, "Well, I guess they would gain knowledge and maybe feel a sense of accomplishment because they did it on their own."

That session was the turning point. Luis began to ask each salesperson a simple question each time he was asked for help: "How would you handle the problem if I weren't here?" He found his people had plenty of answers. It wasn't that they needed him to solve their problems. They had learned that it was easier to get Luis to fix it rather than take the time to do it themselves.

Asking that one question gave Luis 40% more time in the

course of his work week. Just as important, the question helped his people grow again.

Our coaching sessions gave Luis a new perspective on his job as sales manager and created a new experience for his salespeople. He had low situational awareness prior to our coaching discussion. After those talks, he found new ways to help his people succeed.

SANDLER COACHING INSIGHT

Coaching unlocks knowledge that already exists in salespeople and empowers them to better utilize it during their sales day. From the coaching process, salespeople begin to experience their true potential since growth then comes from within.

ENVIRONMENT

As I have noted, the coach is personally responsible for creating the environment necessary for the coaching process to be successful. Far too many managers believe that "coaching on the fly"—which is what Luis believed himself to be doing—is effective. Not only is it ineffective, it's not even coaching, because it fails to create such an environment.

I have seen many salespeople approach a sales manager with the question Luis's people had learned to pose while standing in his doorway: "Do you have a minute?" Once the manager says, "Sure," the salesperson explains a problem he is having and the manager explains how to resolve it. Both parties leave the meeting with a sense of resolution. Yet the real problem remains unsolved. The manager never arrived at the root of the issue: the environment for a coaching session was never created!

Here's the reality. You can't coach someone in a 30-second conversation that takes place in a cubicle, a hallway, or while the person is hovering near the entrance of your office.

To create a proper environment, the coach should ideally schedule a 30-minute meeting in a private room where both parties are comfortable. It is not always possible to commit to thirty minutes for all issues, but a formal process is still effective if used with a shorter timeframe. At any rate, no coaching session should be scheduled for less than fifteen uninterrupted minutes since it cannot be effective in any shorter timeframe.

The meeting should be free from interruptions and have a focused approach, thanks to the coaching contract discussed in the previous chapter. The session should have a relaxed atmosphere where the coach and salesperson exchange information without outside pressure. The environment should feel casual, but note that this is not the same as unstructured. The coach should follow a proven methodology—the seven-step coaching methodology outlined in this chapter—and customize it in such a way as to include the right balance of strategic and tactical coaching and to fit the salesperson's personality.

STRATEGIC AND TACTICAL COACHING

Successful coaches utilize two forms of coaching: **strategic** and **tactical**. Both are essential if the coaching process is to be effective. Strategic coaching helps the salesperson think differently and plan for success more effectively. Tactical coaching, on the other hand, is focused on better execution of the current skill set. It is up to the coach to decide which element is the starting point for growth.

Strategic Coaching

Strategic coaching concentrates on better thinking and planning for success. The focus of this kind of coaching is to aid the salesperson in thinking about the future and the development of a plan to deal with minor issues before they become major problems.

Imagine you're going for a hike. Along the way, you see a mountain range on the horizon. The mountain range looks small in the distance, but as you get closer, the true size of the mountains become more evident. Solving problems or dealing with issues in the future is much the same. For the salesperson who is able to anticipate problems, it's easier to deal with them in the present when their potential impact is relatively small.

Think of strategic coaching as a "force field" where future issues are brought into the present and dealt with before they become too big. The process helps salespeople think on a much larger plane than the one in which the problem currently exists.

Essentially, the effective coach helps the salesperson broaden his vision and deal with sales issues early on, before they evolve into having major negative impact. Let me share a true story that illustrates just how important this kind of coaching can be.

Tom's Story

A sales manager named Tom asked me to help him deal with some serious sales issues that were keeping his team from achieving their volume goals. Tom's salespeople had developed the bad habit of lowering their monthly sales forecast during the third week of each month. This reoccurring problem frustrated Tom since he then had to advise his boss in the weekly company meeting, suffer the negative comments of his colleagues, and, last but not least, deal with the countless long-term effects of sudden sales breakdowns that undermined the long-term income targets for both the department and its team members.

Tom had worked with the sales team as a group on various ways to improve their closing tactics and had reminded them via email to prospect aggressively to avoid this issue. But the problem kept recurring.

During one of our sessions, I had Tom write a statement describing the problem he faced in the center of a blank sheet of paper. It read, "Team lowers forecasts at the end of each month." Then I asked him to draw a big circle around the statement. Next, I had Tom create a list of all the roadblocks he heard from his salespeople over the course of the month that negatively impacted their ability to achieve quota. Lastly, I advised him to arrange face-to-face coaching sessions during the early weeks of the month to help his salespeople "see" the issues they could face later in the month and develop a plan to overcome those problems prior to experiencing them. These one-on-one coaching conversations helped his people better prepare to succeed—instead of focusing on the issue when it was too late to deal with it.

Tactical Coaching

Tactical coaching is very different from strategic coaching, although the two complement and complete each other.

Tactical coaching helps the salesperson improve performance of specific selling behaviors in the context of the job. In order for this type of coaching to be successful, the coach should be prepared to develop a success profile to use as a performance guideline for growth. This profile should detail the specific behaviors necessary for success within the position. (See Chapter One's discussion of the top ten behaviors every field salesperson should be able to execute, which is a good starting point.) This list of behaviors then morphs into a more detailed job description and quantifies the expectations for execution.

A typical job description is an overview of the expectations for the position combined with the top ten behaviors as well as the key performance indicators. The overview is a big picture of the position. The job description for an outside sales position would detail the territory and the types of accounts called on, as well as the results of the selling efforts. It further would describe the process of achieving quota and the methodology used when performing the function. The next part of the job description would detail the top ten behaviors to be performed and the expected results from each behavior. The last part of the job description is an overview the key performance indicators used to judge the person as successful in the position.

Additionally, as I've mentioned earlier in this book, the salesperson must already have been trained in the proper implementation of all behaviors. To this end, the salesperson should have created a behavior Cookbook for Success outlining the numeric expectation for each behavior.

Tactical coaching is designed to help the salesperson better understand the short-term impact of the behavior he is performing and the skills he is applying—the direct effect of what he's actually doing on the outcome of his sales calls. As I suggested earlier in the book, there is a danger associated with tactical coaching. It has the potential to evolve into training, and coaching and training are two very different roles.

If those two roles are not separated, the coach may inadvertently become trainer, teaching new skills during the session. Although this may seem like a good idea, it's actually counterproductive because it is a re-teaching of training that has already taken place, creating learned helplessness. To guard against this, the coach must focus on helping the salesperson better use the skills already in place to improve results. Tactical coaching is usually focused on briefing or debriefing sales calls and conducting role-plays that involve a buyer/seller situation in which the coach can witness the sale from the salesperson's perspective.

Aliyah's Story

Aliyah is a 5-year sales veteran in the printing industry who, upon returning from a disastrous sales call, asked Vincent, her manager, for a coaching session. Her manager saw the concern on Aliyah's face. The two set aside half an hour and went to a quiet conference room where they wouldn't be interrupted.

Vincent asked Aliyah to "play the movie" of the events she remembered leading up to as well as during the sales call. Aliyah slowly reviewed the events as though they were a movie playing in slow motion, frame by frame. This helped Vincent understand where Aliyah veered from the path to success. Vincent slowed the movie to a crawl in order to fully understand all the problematic issues. This was far preferable to a rapid-fire review that leaves out important details.

During the coaching session, through the skillful use of advanced questioning strategies, as discussed in Chapter Eight of this book, Vincent determined the cause of Aliyah's issue. A weak up-front contract had caused Aliyah to use features and benefits in the attempt to get the prospect interested. Aliyah didn't see the impact of this mistake on her sales call until Vincent's questions pointed it out.

Play the Movie

Whenever a coach is involved in tactical coaching, it is important to help the salesperson see the problem by walking him through the event in a slow methodical process. Do what Vincent did: Play the movie in slow motion, and stop it at critical moments.

Questions like, "What was your strategy?" "What Sandler tactics did you apply?" "And then what happened?" and "What did you do next?" are key exploratory phrases. The coach should ask questions like these frequently so the salesperson doesn't leave out any important details. The coach has to probe the specific Sandler selling skills used during the sales call to help the salesperson better understand more effective ways to apply them in the future. In Aliyah's case, Vincent had her recreate her up-front contract during a role-play in minute detail so he could review the elements as well as the tonality she had used in delivering it. This helped to uncover an important "miss" by Aliyah and gave Vincent a chance to review her understanding of the specific elements of the up-front contract—and its importance to the sales call that followed.

THE SANDLER COACHING SYSTEM

The Sandler Coaching System allows a manager to approach each coaching session with a strategic direction that can be customized for each salesperson and developed into a personalized coaching style. This methodology is based on seven distinct steps I'll be sharing in just a moment.

Using this methodology prevents managers from falling into the trap of coaching salespeople in the same manner as they personally like to be coached. The Sandler coaching methodology raises coaching from the level of informal conversation to effective behavior and attitude transformation.

KARI'S STORY

Kari is a manager who strongly believes in the power of coaching. Over the years, she has cobbled together thoughts from different coaching books she's read and used them as her guides. During sessions with her salespeople, she has often found herself jumping from topic to topic, using more of an intuitive process than a specific coaching formula. Eventually, she became frustrated when her tactics didn't work.

Her intentions were correct, but the psychology behind each action she took was missing so her coaching process was flawed. She never got around to digging deep enough to find the real issues inhibiting a team member's success. Once she did, her team's performance improved.

Like a lot of managers, Kari was trying to "reinvent the wheel" when it comes to coaching salespeople. Many managers believe in coaching their salespeople and spend a great deal of time trying to perfect their methodology. Few can point to any consistent record of success. The Sandler Coaching System, on the other hand, is a proven seven-step process with a long record of transforming sales careers and turning around departments that find themselves in trouble. It gives the coach a formal, step-by-step process for success, similar to the Sandler system—the familiar Sandler Submarine, with its seven compartments for Bonding & Rapport, Up-Front Contracts, Pain, Budget, Decision, Fulfillment, and Post-Sell—does. (For more information on the Sandler system, see David Sandler's book, *You Can't Teach a Kid to Ride a Bike at a Seminar.*)

THE SEVEN-STEP SANDLER COACHING SYSTEM METHODOLOGY

There are seven steps in the Sandler coaching methodology. Each of these steps must be executed in order, in a sequence that builds from what has gone before. Notice that the methodology employs a "feedback loop" strategy between manager and salesperson as its core principle. You'll learn more about this strategy in Chapter Eight.

1. **Assess Current Status:** In this initial step, the coach diagnoses the current business situation, evaluates the salesperson's competency, benchmarks the timeline for success, and establishes the specific coaching structure to be utilized. The coach observes the salesperson describe the coaching issue and looks for any awareness the salesperson may or may not have regarding the actions being taken as well as their impact. In the assessment step, the coach begins to understand the depth and complexity of the problem and

starts to formulate a coaching plan and a timeline. The coach utilizes the Devine Inventory and DISC evaluations to assess the hidden competency as well as the behavioral tendencies of the salesperson. These evaluations help the effective coach customize the coaching process to address the salesperson in a more personalized, precise manner. The coach needs to set a strong coaching up-front contract designed to explore all the comments made in the evaluation and the implications they have on the salesperson's success. The contract used here is the same coaching contract the coach established with the salesperson at the beginning of the coaching process.

2. **Establish Growth Goals:** During this step, the coach works with the salesperson to set expectations for the coaching process as well as create goals used in measuring success. The coaching contract is developed, and the rules of engagement are made clear to both the coach and salesperson. Some of the coaching goals will be short-term to gain momentum and traction, while others will be long-term.

3. **Define New Behavior:** In the third step of the coaching process, the coach explores new behaviors. This means working with the salesperson to better utilize existing skills in need of improvement. This focus on behavior modification is the result of awareness garnered from the assessment phase of coaching. For example, a salesperson who

consistently falls short of sales quotas may discover he has a weak pipeline of new opportunity. Instead of simply focusing on making more cold calls to fill the pipeline, the coach helps the salesperson recognize the need for the addition of networking, referrals, and business-introduction behaviors to his Cookbook for Success. These new behaviors improve the quality of the leads generated, which has a direct influence on the salesperson's closing rate.

4. **Execute New Behavior:** This step involves the execution of the new behavior plan, as well as the corresponding skills, as part of the sales plan. This requires an implementation plan and commitment from the salesperson to work on the new behavior for twenty consecutive days in order to form a new habit. The 20-day standard is not arbitrary. Many salespeople lose momentum and develop a false sense of success about the thirteenth day so they stop working on the new behavior and slide back into the bad behavior patterns that created problems. During this step, the salesperson keeps a behavioral journal for the entire twenty days to track positive or negative patterns and record both successes and failures.

5. **Review Progress:** The fifth step of coaching involves regular check-ins on the timeline developed in the assessment phase. Simple issues or problems may take a little time to correct, while major problems will likely need a series of coaching sessions. The manager must follow up with

the salesperson to maintain momentum since slippage is possible due to performance pressure. If the new behavior isn't dealing with the problem effectively, further coaching or a totally new approach may be necessary. The Sandler Success Triangle, formed by connecting behavior, attitude, and technique, is the perfect strategy to utilize during these check-ins. The coach should review the behavior performed to determine whether or not it is achieving the goal, analyze the impact of the new behavior on the salesperson's attitude, and examine the techniques executed in the performance of the new behavior. Role-play is a very effective tool in this phase.

6. **Modify Behavior:** In many cases, the new behavior needs to be assessed and adjusted to better address the salesperson's abilities. The sixth step is therefore designed to recalibrate behavior in order to pursue the goal more effectively. "More, better, and different" are the three variables to be considered at this time.

   • Does the salesperson have to perform **more** behavior to achieve the goal? For this variable, the coach and salesperson determine that the behavior is correct; however, the salesperson is not performing enough of it so it should be increased. Example: Twenty-five cold calls per day instead of five.

   • Does the salesperson have to perform the new behavior in a **better** way than he currently is in order to accomplish the goal? For this variable, the salesperson and coach determine the salesperson needs to improve on the quality of the behavior performed. Example: The salesperson needs to set a stronger up-front contract with prospects instead of the weak one he is currently setting.

- Lastly, does the coach have to create a totally **different** behavior model to accomplish the goal? For this variable, the salesperson needs to execute a completely different behavior from the current one he is utilizing. Example: Instead of relying on cold calling, the salesperson should focus on networking, referrals, and business introductions to be more effective at prospecting.

This "more, better, or different" approach discussed earlier in this book places success squarely in the hands of the salesperson.

7. **Evaluate Success:** The last step of the Sandler coaching methodology is focused on gauging whether or not coaching is achieving sustainable success. This step is referred to as "success mapping," since it establishes a behavioral map designed to be utilized by the salesperson to achieve the coaching goal and prevent the problem from reoccurring in the future. The salesperson must maintain behavioral momentum for the next ninety days in order to imprint success and anchor growth. Once again, the behavior

journal plays a key role. The salesperson records daily progress by writing a short plan each morning prior to beginning the day. This plan should detail the specific behavior to be performed during the course of the day. At the end of the day, the salesperson should write a debrief report outlining all accomplishments. This creates a success map for ninety days and reinforces the growth and development that is taking place.

Seven-Step Sandler Coaching System

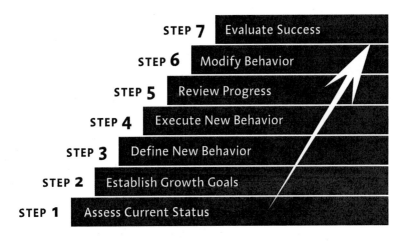

Here's an example of an entry in the behavior journal.

November 15

5:30 A.M.

I have been struggling with prospecting consistently so my sales volume has been mercurial—rising and falling. I feel tremendous pressure from my manager as I report my sales for the week since some weeks have very low sales volume. Today, I will build time blocks into my online calendar and space my prospecting throughout the day instead of trying to jam it all into the morning. This is important as it allows me to brief and debrief each call. I will create three distinct time blocks for cold calling using the optimum time when decision makers should answer their phone. The time blocks are 7:30 to 9:00 A.M., 11:00 A.M. to 12:30 P.M. and 4:00 to 5:30 P.M.

6:00 P.M.

My new plan was more comfortable, and I felt relaxed during my calls. I reached five decision makers from the twenty-five dials I made, which is four more than usual. Day 1 of my 20-day goal has begun on a high note, and I look forward to tomorrow's dials. I feel more confident in being able to improve my cold calling success rate, which translates into a better phone presence during the call.

See also Chapter Ten, which offers insights on how to analyze a journal entry.

A CONTINUOUS COACHING LOOP

The seven steps of the Sandler Coaching System form a development loop providing continuous learning and growth for the salesperson. This loop helps both the salesperson and the manager understand the importance of each individual step in the process. Both parties understand how the seven steps fit together to create success, much like the compartments in the Sandler Submarine.

With large sales forces, it is almost impossible for a single manager to use this methodology on all members of the team. The Devine Inventory and DISC evaluations play an important role, helping the manager understand the more immediate needs of the team. Selling performance, quote attainment, observation, feedback, and key performance indicators also play an important role in creating a ranking of individual coaching needs. This ranking of individual salespeople in the sales force creates a priority coaching list. The manager can then focus on those salespeople with the greatest potential to grow, rather than defaulting to spending too much time with the bottom 20%, who are more likely to give lip service to the goal of personal growth. Additionally, the ranking creates a 20/60/20 list (see Chapter Four) that the manager can use as a guide for making the greatest impact on the team. Working with each segment in a way that best suits their willingness to grow helps managers set specific goals based on the 20/60/20 designation. The top 20% need nurturing and recognition, the middle 60% need small goals to give them traction, and the bottom 20% need to prove they are worthy of time by making dramatic behavioral shifts and moving out of their comfort zone.

The loop can also be used by the salespeople, on their own, as a self-coaching tool. It is not unusual to find high-performing salespeople using the coaching process on themselves or with a peer to accelerate their growth or work on specific problems.

Individual members of the team may excel in one or more areas of the Sandler Selling System, and they may be able to perform coaching duties in the areas in which they shine. Developing these internal coaches takes pressure off the manager and builds an in-house team of coaches who can have a strong impact on the progress of the team. These internal coaches must be cautioned to avoid the training/coaching trap in which they lapse into teaching skills the salesperson already has but is afraid to execute.

SANDLER COACHING RULES

- Take full responsibility for creating a positive coaching experience and environment for the session.

- Use strategic coaching first to help salespeople plan to succeed and tactical coaching next to work on specific issues of execution.

- Follow the seven steps in the Sandler Coaching System in the order they are given since each builds off the previous step.

- Encourage self-coaching and peer-to-peer coaching as a way to accelerate growth.

CHAPTER SEVEN

Understanding Salespeople

OVERVIEW

- The *why* of success
- Coaching the four types of salespeople
- Motivation and habit
- Exploring assets and liabilities

In this chapter, you will learn ways to access the salesperson's personal motivation for changing behavior and raising his performance. Coaching fails whenever the coach takes ownership of the salesperson's growth—instead of using coaching to ignite the salesperson's personal passion.

THE *WHY* OF SUCCESS

Every salesperson has a personal *why* buried behind each of the behaviors he performs. This is the inner voice motivating the choices made throughout the sales day. This *why* is unique to each salesperson. It becomes a personal North Star, directing the choices that salesperson makes.

SOPHIA'S STORY

During an executive coaching session, I asked Sophia, the CEO of a Fortune 1000 company, why she believed her salespeople showed up at work each day. At first, she was puzzled by the question. I assured her that I was serious and waited patiently for her reply.

After some quiet introspection, she responded, "Money and recognition."

I asked, "Why do you think that?"

She beamed and said, "Because that's how I would answer the question!" When I asked how sure she was they would give the same answer, she looked at me for a long time and then said she would have to find out.

She surveyed her sales force anonymously. Only about 25% responded to the same question with the answer "money and rec-ognition." Another 65% responded with something that shocked her to learn. Nearly two-thirds of her sales force said the number one reason they showed up for work was "security"!

Sophia had no idea that the majority of her sales force was

driven by the comfort and perceived stability of working for a large company—not by the drivers of selling success that motivated her.

WHAT MOTIVATES YOU DOESN'T NECESSARILY MOTIVATE OTHERS

Sophia learned an important lesson about salespeople, one that all high-performing coaches understand: What motivates one person is not what motivates another. When it comes to motivation, it pays to remember that salespeople are unique human beings.

To motivate a salesperson toward higher performance, you must understand those factors that motivate that individual. You can't assume they are the same factors that motivate you. **What** (the goal or purpose of the coaching process), **why** (the unique reason for the salesperson to change behavior), and **impact** (what happens if the behavior pattern doesn't change) are the three critical areas every coach must explore, in the course of a coaching session, to support constructive change.

For now, let's not get distracted by *what* and *impact*, two topics that sometimes lead the coaching sessions of ineffective coaches. Each salesperson has a subjective and intimate *why* that is so unique that the coach first must be skilled enough to identify and access it. If the coach can't do that, it will be impossible to help the salesperson grow.

The *why* is the emotion that brings the *what* and the *impact*. That's what you want to address first. The *what* typically focuses on the goal or purpose of the coaching process, and the *impact* is usually what happens when the salesperson understands what he should be doing at the end of the coaching process. However, the *why* is the connector or personal reason each salesperson must make the necessary changes.

High-performing salespeople change when the pain of remaining the same is greater than the pain involved in making the change. Lower performers, by contrast, may wallow in their pain and use it as an excuse to not even try. This dynamic is central to understanding the *why* connection to coaching effectiveness. Without it, coaching becomes an intellectual exercise with no reason to act.

The *why* ignites the inner drive within salespeople and becomes the rocket fuel behind the behavioral changes salespeople must make. You must have noticed that some salespeople are more passionate about their profession than others. Those are the ones who have harnessed the power of *why*. Behavior without *why* is intellectual and ineffective.

I utilize the 5 Whys questioning strategy developed by the Japanese inventor, Sakichi Toyoda. Toyoda's premise revolves around asking five consecutive *why* questions about any problem or issue, in order to determine the root cause of it. Each *why* probes a deeper layer of the issue and helps the questioner fully understand the real problem.

Let's examine a typical scenario involving a coach and salesperson, and see how the 5 Whys approach raises the quality of the information in the discussion for both parties.

Salesperson: "I'm struggling with my cold calls."

Coach: "Why?"

Salesperson: "I'm not comfortable on the phone."

Coach: "Why?"

Salesperson: "I feel like I'm a nuisance when I call."

Coach: "Why?"

Salesperson: "Well, when salespeople call me, they are interrupting my work time."

Coach: "Why?"

Salesperson: "Because they immediately try to sell me without having a relationship."

Coach: "Why?"

Salesperson: "I guess they haven't been taught the importance of bonding and rapport."

Coach: "So what does that mean?"

Salesperson: "Maybe I should focus more on building a relationship during my first call to help prospects understand that I'm different from the typical salesperson who calls them."

THE 5 WHYS

WHY? *I'm struggling with my cold calls.*

WHY? *I'm not comfortable on the phone.* ICEBERG

WHY? *I feel like a nuisance when I call.*

WHY? *When I get sales calls on the phone my workday is interrupted.*

WHY? *Because they immediately try to sell me something.*

I guess they haven't been taught the importance of bonding and rapport.

In this case, the coach helped the salesperson deal with the real issue without resorting to teaching cold-calling techniques. Each *why* probed a deeper layer and uncovered a critical belief embedded in the salesperson's mind. Successful coaches understand the importance of peeling back the onion in this way to get to the core of the issue.

COACHING THE FOUR TYPES OF SALESPEOPLE

Coaching is not a "one size fits all" undertaking. It must be customized to fit the characteristics and attributes of each salesperson. To this end, the sales manager must be aware of four personality types likely to be encountered on the sales team. Each requires a different approach during the coaching session.

Self-Taught

The individual with the self-taught personality type has utilized the trial and error method to improve selling effectiveness. Self-taught salespeople typically grow by eliminating costly errors over time, which means progress is slow. The self-taught salesperson often doesn't want to follow the Sandler system even when he has been trained to do so because old habits have become comfortable. Such salespeople usually achieve sporadic success due to a lot of "fits and starts."

The effective coach must first make sure this salesperson is trained in the strategies and tactics of the Sandler system. Without this critical skill set training, it is impossible to work on either knowledge or application. This salesperson must, at the very least, attend a Sandler boot camp or Foundations program as this will provide a baseline for coaching. Next, the coach should begin coaching the importance of the key elements of the system: relationship building, qualifying, closing, presenting, and questioning. Once this has been accomplished, sustainable growth can by attained through improving the usage of the Sandler Selling System.

The Renegade

This individual lives by the creed, "I like to do things my way!" and fights utilizing the Sandler system in its entirety. Renegades are constantly experimenting with strategies other than the Sandler system. They tend to have "streaky" success patterns, with long periods of failure when nothing seems to work. They may resist the Sandler system, claiming it is "too robotic and confining." As a result, they find themselves at the mercy of the prospect's system (mislead, steal expertise, mislead again, and hide).

This personality style is the most difficult to coach. In many cases, knowledge of the Sandler system is present; however, the salesperson chooses not to use it. The effective coach's main job is to raise the awareness of the Sandler selling strategies—not the specific tactics—and how these strategies help avoid the traps set by the prospect. This salesperson should be guided to set small goals designed to build traction and gain little selling victories.

The Player

This personality type believes in "natural ability" and relies heavily on personality and intuition to gain selling success. Such salespeople, after being trained in the Sandler Selling System, typically use a lighter, highly "customized" version of the system, frequently leaving out key strategies and tactics that don't "feel right." When they are lucky enough to find themselves in front of prospects who are willing to be schmoozed, they may succeed; however, they rely heavily on their expense account and entertainment budget to get the job done. This type is often called the "professional visitor" as these salespeople make a lot of sales calls designed to make the prospect know and like them.

Since these salespeople rely on personality, it is important for the coach to help them incorporate their personality in the Sandler system. Personalization of the Sandler strategies and tactics is the key to greater usage and success.

The Continuous Learner

Upon completing training, this type of individual totally accepts the Sandler strategies and tactics as the pathway to success. Continuous learners are open to coaching and recognize the power of briefing and debriefing sales calls. They are adept at problem solving when they encounter a difficult business situation. Their growth is consistent and sustainable; they are always striving to improve their effectiveness. Continuous learners are goal setters with enough self-awareness to understand what's happening in a sales call, and they use the effective coach to work on specific issues that are standing in the way of greater success.

These salespeople have already bought into the need for the Sandler Selling System so the coaching goal is to improve effectiveness when they are using it. This coaching style centers on visualization of the specific events associated with the issue or problem. The coaching session is a review of the sales call as if it were a movie run in frame-by-frame slow motion. The effective coach utilizes active listening and open-ended questions to review each frame. Phrases like, "Then what happened?," "Tell me more," and "What happened next?" are key to the salesperson's memory of the events. Once awareness is triggered, the salesperson can begin to use knowledge of the Sandler strategies and tactics to resolve the issue.

WITH WHICH OF THE FOUR ARE YOU WORKING?

It is important to categorize the salesperson in one of the preceding four types as a starting point for the coaching process. The coach then can review the behavior performed in the sales call, discover the roadblocks, and focus on the coaching style most likely to achieve success.

SANDLER COACHING INSIGHT

I should share some insights on a new generation of salespeople who will eventually dominate the selling profession: the Millennials. Few of the Millennial salespeople I
work with are wholly motivated by money, and social acceptance is usually the driving factor in their success. Recognition is a powerful motivator for these professionals,
and quality of life is extremely important to their sales
day. Companies employing this workforce successfully
create a low-key, fun atmosphere where productivity is
an offshoot of the social environment. This new breed of
sales superstars are accustomed to the product or service
they sell having a lot of cache so they are likely to focus on
features and benefits to close the sale.

Coaching Millennials effectively usually takes the form
of mentoring during the session. The coach must model
the behavioral and attitudinal changes the Millennial
salesperson is to incorporate. The coach must use a
more casual style during the coaching process and be
less regimented in approach, without sacrificing the
Sandler Coaching System methodology. The coach must
also show personal interest in the salesperson's life
as a balance to the focus on job improvement. Coaching must relate to the Millennials' world, and provide a
"soft bottom" when they struggle. Remember: Millennial salespeople were raised in an era where everyone
received a trophy just for competing! It's particularly
important to coach these contributors to be the best
version of themselves. Coaching them to be "number
one on the sales team" may backfire.

?
WHAT DOES IT MEAN?

● **Millennials** are part of the large U.S. demographic cohort following Generation X (born after 1965). Complicating discussions of the Millennial group is the reality that there are no commonly accepted dates describing when this generation starts and ends. Analysts use birth years that can go all the way from the early 1980s to the early 2000s. Generalizations are dangerous with any demographic group, but common traits that have been widely noted among Millennials include deep familiarity with communications technology, strong social orientation, and a blurring of the lines between work and play.

MOTIVATION AND HABIT

It's important for the coach to fully understand the personal motivation of the salesperson. This is essential to the achievement of greater levels of success. In higher-performing salespeople, the motivation is typically driven by a desire to achieve at a new "personal best" level and to earn more money or recognition. Unfortunately, in lower performers, the motivation is usually job security and comfort, two motivators that tend to accompany mediocre financial results.

There is a critical link between motivation and habit. Motivation is the starting point for success; habit is the sustaining point of success.

MIKE'S STORY; SANTIAGO'S STORY

Mike is a salesman with a 10-year track record of mediocrity at the same firm. His company was recently purchased. The new owners asked me to help them manage turnover on the sales team to improve their overall performance. After much soul searching, Mike determined that he needed to improve his production—for the simple reason that he wanted to keep his job.

Mike presented himself to me as someone who, as he said, "saw the light" and was willing to "do what it takes to be successful." I helped him develop a behavioral map to raise his performance and coached him on handling his most difficult selling situations.

Mike started strong, making all the changes I had recommended, but he quickly slipped back to his old ways and was terminated after forty-five days. Mike failed not because he didn't know what to do, but because his motivation wasn't strong enough to sustain the behavioral changes he needed to lock in. He resorted to his old excuses—and failed.

Santiago, a salesperson with the same company, had a similar meeting with me as he, too, was an "upper 60%-er" on his sales team. Santiago's goal—to remain employed—was the same as Mike's. Unlike Mike, however, Santiago realized that locking in the changes necessary to improve his performance would take time. Santiago and I built a series of small goals to be achieved over the first twenty days of our coaching relationship, and he used the attainment of these goals as "mile markers" on a roadmap to the success he craved.

Greater success came in small steps, each one building on the previous one. He did not make excuses, and he did not fall back into old, unproductive habits. At the end of forty-five days, Santiago's sales manager observed Santiago's commitment to success and worked with him closely—and successfully—to sustain it.

Both Mike and Santiago had similar motivation initially, but Santiago turned his motivation into a more productive set of habits with the help of his coach and manager. Mike fell back on what was familiar—and self-destructed. The lesson here is clear: Motivation alone is not enough to grow, but motivation turned into habit is. The coach needs to understand the personal motivation each salesperson brings to the coaching process and then aid the salesperson in developing higher-performing habits to turn that motivation into reality.

ASSETS AND LIABILITIES

All salespeople have external strengths and weaknesses, visible to those around them, as well as internal strengths and weaknesses that are hidden from sight. All of these must be understood if the salesperson is to change and grow. These attributes become personal assets and liabilities. They either aid the salesperson's growth or inhibit it.

Failure to understand the impact of these issues can give the coach a false sense of progress. All too often, the salesperson seems to be moving in the right direction only to slide back to old, unproductive patterns of behavior.

SKYLAR'S STORY

Skylar is a financial planner who works for a mid-size brokerage company. She has shown moderate success and her sales manager Al feels she has the talent to achieve greater success than she has in the past. Al has used ongoing coaching sessions to help Skylar become more effective at closing business when she is in front of prospects. She seems to have a strong desire to improve, but for some reason she continues to struggle.

Skylar follows the Sandler Selling System taught in her weekly classes. During one of her classes, she learned about the importance of finding pain instead of relying on features and benefits and began using this approach immediately to explore her prospects' need for her services. After a month of application, though, Skylar's sales results remained unchanged. She became frustrated.

Al came to me for help, and I agreed to conduct coaching sessions with Skylar. After just a single meeting, I was able to determine that she was being held back by her need to be liked by the prospect and her emotional attachment to the result of her sales calls. I discovered that she did, in fact, ask pain exploration questions—but she watered them down so as not to make her prospect uncomfortable. She did this out of a deep-seated fear that prospects wouldn't like her anymore.

Skylar was using the Sandler system, but she needed help to realize that an inner fear was holding her back from greater effectiveness. She needed to do an inventory of her own assets and liabilities. Once she did this, her performance improved.

CONDUCT AN INVENTORY

Take the time now to familiarize yourself with some of the key assets and liabilities the coach typically has to examine to determine how to help salespeople develop to their full potential.

Assets

Assets are behaviors that have a positive impact on the salesperson if they are present and consistently utilized. The coach may use these behaviors during sessions with salespeople to help them achieve greater success. Bear in mind that all salespeople have internal thought patterns and behavioral patterns they repeat, whether these patterns are productive or not. The big question is whether these thought and behavioral patterns can be noticed.

The following are five key assets that, if present, make coaching success more likely.

1. **Awareness:** There are two critical forms of awareness: self and situational. Self-awareness is important as it helps salespeople objectively brief and debrief behavior and analyze the role they have personally played in their success or failure. A salesperson with high self-awareness always looks inward first to gain insight prior to examining the external factors surrounding the event. The coach

must advise those salespeople who are hypervigilant not to become overly critical of themselves since this can have a negative impact on their concept of Identity and can inhibit their growth. Situational awareness, on the other hand, helps salespeople analyze cause and effect—the reasons for and consequences of their actions. The coach should help salespeople with high situational awareness understand the impact of their actions on the present as well as future sales calls.

2. **Goals**: A salesperson's commitment to the goal-setting process is a key asset since it develops a map for him to follow as he grows. Salespeople tend to grow in the direction of the goals they set so the coach should fully understand their goals or help develop goals necessary for growth. It is almost impossible to successfully coach a salesperson who doesn't set goals. Goal setters typically outperform problem solvers because they align their goals with their purpose.

3. **Structure**: Salespeople who naturally create structure and methodology are building a success track on which the coach can establish growth and development markers. These markers are similar to the mileposts you see along the highway, indicating the distance you have travelled. Structure helps the salesperson and coach organize critical behavior necessary for sustained, measurable growth.

4. **Thinking**: I place a high value on a salesperson's ability to

think strategically. Far too many salespeople, in my view, place a higher value on immediate action rather than on strategic thinking. Memory is built when salespeople take their time to develop strategically sound, well-thought-out behaviors; the coach must help the salesperson build "muscle memory" in the brain so the behaviors executed are easily repeatable. One of my favorite coaching questions is, "What was the reason behind such-and-such behavior?" You would be surprised how many times I receive the response, "I'm not sure!" Coaches can help salespeople raise their awareness by utilizing the 5 Whys, a tactic I mentioned earlier.

5. **Time:** Salespeople are always in a rush to make something happen. Time becomes an asset if used properly or a liability if not. There are only so many productive hours in a day—salespeople must make intelligent choices about where and how they are going to invest the available time. The coach has to help salespeople understand the "slow down to speed up" rule. No one wins a marathon by sprinting the entire 26.2 miles. There is a pace associated with growth, just as there is a pace for a winning marathon runner. The coach must help the salesperson establish a realistic pace for growth—too fast and the salesperson crashes; too slow and the salesperson becomes unproductive.

Liabilities

Liabilities are attributes that adversely impact a salesperson's success. Often, they are both hidden and hardwired. If not dealt with, over time they cause repeatable problems that negatively impact coaching success. Here are the top five liabilities I have encountered in my coaching sessions.

1. **Need for approval:** In many cases a salesperson's self-worth is derived from what prospects think of him, which may breed insecurity prospects can exploit to get what they want. A salesperson with a high need for approval will never ask prospects the tough questions for fear of being disliked. The coach must help the salesperson understand a basic fact embedded in the buyer-seller relationship: selling has nothing to do with being liked by the prospect; rather, it has everything to do with being respected by the prospect. Additionally, the coach must help salespeople develop a bulletproof mentality by helping them get their approval needs met in their personal life. A well-balanced personal and professional life is key to breaking the dependency caused by the approval trap. This is why the coach must help the salesperson grow in each area of life.

2. **Outlook:** Many people view the world around them as either positive or negative, and this view molds their outlook. Salespeople who have a positive, pragmatic, reality-based outlook tend to achieve more than the ones

who have a negative one since positive salespeople tend to accept more challenges, believing they will succeed. Negative salespeople, by contrast, always seem to find a reason to justify not taking action. The coach will find it much easier to work with positive salespeople than negative ones since salespeople with a positive outlook tend to have an openness to "What if you tried...?" coaching strategies and are willing to risk failure. The coach should feed the positive nature by helping all members of the sales team stretch beyond their current reach. Salespeople with a negative outlook must be motivated—tactfully—to set goals that test the validity of their negative beliefs and to chart a new course of action when that is warranted. This is not to suggest that salespeople with a positive outlook present no coaching challenges. Salespeople with extremely positive outlooks tend to develop "happy ears"—meaning they assume positive outcomes where there is no evidence for them—and may believe they can turn everything a prospect says into a positive. This is unrealistic, and the coach has to help connect the positive outlook to realistic outcomes. In both cases, the salesperson's outlook must be tempered with reality.

3. **Emotion:** Unchecked emotion, either high or low, can cause issues. The salesperson must demonstrate composure in the face of the inevitable selling challenges. When salespeople lose composure, they tend to heap more

mistakes on top of the ones they may have already made. The coach must help the salesperson develop a strategy to regain composure after any negative occurrence on the sales call. Without this habit, one problem may build on another until a situation that could have been resolved without much difficulty becomes a full-fledged disaster. The first step the coach typically takes is to work with the salesperson on not dwelling on the mistake or magnifying it to unrealistic proportions. Next, the coach has to help the salesperson reframe the mistake into a learning opportunity. Finally, the coach must help the salesperson focus on what should happen next in order to develop positive, forward thinking.

4. **Fear of rejection:** The fear of rejection is a real success-killer in sales. It stems from the sensations salespeople experience when they are in a situation in which a prospect may reject one of their thoughts or proposals. In the salesperson's mind, this may become more than the simple rejection of an idea, but instead a rejection of him personally. This perceived personal rejection causes the salesperson to recoil and makes him act tentatively around prospects in general. The avoidance of any situation where *no* is a possible outcome raises anxiety and drives a lot of "think-it-overs" with no closing over time. The coach has to help the salesperson reframe the rejection experience. In prospecting, for example, the salesperson should be

encouraged to collect *no* responses instead of *yeses*—with the thought, "It takes a certain numbers of *noes* to get a *yes,* and each *no* brings me closer to a *yes.*"

5. **Ego:** Of course, it is important for the salesperson to maintain a self-assured attitude in front of the prospect. But questions of balance must be considered. Overly confident salespeople are viewed as cocky or arrogant, and those with low confidence are viewed as weak. If ego were measured on a 1 to 10 scale, the ideal sales ego score for a salesperson is about a 5. The coach must work with the salesperson to help him gain and display the appropriate level of confidence in order to increase the respect of those around him.

A MESSY BUSINESS

Salespeople are messy, and in many cases unpredictable. It is important for the coach to take the time to understand their key internal drivers to help them develop their true potential. The effective coach should encourage all salespeople to perform a thorough "internal body scan" to raise personal awareness of assets and liabilities. Assessments like those provided by The Devine Group and Extended DISC, in addition to observations of behavior and attitude during the coaching sessions, will aid the coach in developing the personal insights necessary to help the salesperson grow.

SANDLER COACHING RULES

- Access each salesperson's reason or personal *why* behind behavior to help the salesperson grow.
- Understand the four sales personalities to apply the necessary coaching style for success.
- Work to turn the salesperson's motivation into habit.
- Develop critical insight by understanding the salesperson's assets and liabilities since these can drive or inhibit growth.
- Discern the salesperson's internal thought and behavioral patterns, both productive and nonproductive.

CHAPTER EIGHT

The Coach's Toolbox

OVERVIEW

- Effective coaching skills
- Constructive feedback
- Strategic thinking
- The role of journaling

I n this chapter, you will learn to utilize the skills that are critical to creating a successful coaching environment. The effective coach asks questions to make the salesperson think about problems at a much deeper level and provides feedback designed to reinforce all of the learning that takes place during the coaching session.

EFFECTIVE COACHING SKILLS

In order to achieve the desired result of each coaching session, the coach must rely on a well-stocked toolbox. These tools, or skills, help the coach elevate a simple conversation between manager and salesperson to a productive interaction where both parties achieve their goals.

Some of the same questioning skills utilized in the Sandler Selling System methodology prove helpful during the coaching session. This is one of the ways a typical coaching session mirrors a sales call. Advanced questioning strategies such as reversing (answering a question with a question), strip-lining (raising a possibility that is the opposite of what the other person expects to hear from you), active listening (shown by questions and statements indicating you have been listening without an agenda), and the Dummy Curve (which includes asking questions that suggest you might know less than you actually do) can all prove helpful in gathering critical information. These must be employed without the transgression TV legal dramas have warned us about for so many years—leading the witness. During a sales call, these nurturing questioning skills allow the salesperson to dig deep into the prospect's real issues. They can also help the coach move below the surface of the problem to get to the root of the salesperson's issues, too.

THE STORY OF JORDAN AND MILT

Salesperson Jordan was struggling to achieve his monthly quota. He was becoming more and more frustrated with the many proposals he had on the street that were not closing. He was sure he was using the Sandler system properly and that his disappointing results were attributable to a run of bad luck. Milt, his sales manager, asked me to get involved since Jordan's frustration was adversely affecting the team.

I was asked to observe Milt's coaching session with Jordan and debrief with Milt after it concluded. It took only a few minutes for me to confirm that the bulk of the problem lay with Milt's approach to the coaching relationship. As a side note, I should point out here that it's very difficult for sales managers to be part of a coaching session solely as an observer and not comment until the post-coaching session debrief session. We all have the "fix it" gene!

I sat for forty-five minutes while Milt listened to Jordan's version of the events contributing to his current situation. After each explanation, Milt interjected with a comment designed to guide Jordan to the proper solution. I remained silent, taking notes, and watched the interactions carefully so I could provide Milt with good coaching when we met later.

During a role-play, Jordan detailed solid bonding-and-rapport–building strategies, and established a detailed up-front contract. He even found two pains during that critical step of the Sandler methodology and moved skillfully through the

Budget and Decision Steps of the process. When he reached the Fulfillment Step, Jordan made a great presentation, matching his solutions to the prospect's pains. Milt was baffled. On the surface, Jordan was flawlessly performing all aspects of the Sandler system. Milt assumed the problem had to be elsewhere.

I asked Jordan to stay for my debriefing session with Milt as I felt the three of us could have a productive coaching session where both parties would benefit. Jordan and Milt agreed.

I pointed out that, with the exception of the role-play, Milt actually did most of the talking during the coaching session. He asked a few questions, made major assumptions about Jordan's reasons for the steps he took, and offered advice based on those assumptions. These assumptions proved inaccurate. They were not helpful in correcting the problem. Instead of gathering information, Milt gave off-target advice on how to avoid problems Jordan didn't really have.

We replayed the coaching session as if it were a movie in slow motion. Jordan learned an important coaching lesson. Each time Jordan answered his manager's question, I "paused" the manager and had him probe deeper into Jordan's response, using the Sandler questioning strategies: reversing, strip-lining, active listening, and the Dummy Curve. This debrief session proved to be incredibly valuable to Milt because he gathered a significant amount of new information that shed a dramatically different light on Jordan's true issues. Milt determined that Jordan was approaching the Sandler Selling System intellectually. He was using the Sandler system on a surface level and never digging deep into any of the prospect's issues. Initially, Milt was baffled. It seemed Jordan had been doing exactly what he should have been doing. Milt's use of the questioning strategies uncovered true flaws in Jordan's approach—he was not really engaging with the prospect on a personal level.

Jordan's performance turned around. Milt's coaching routine did, too.

FOUR QUESTIONING STRATEGIES

Here's an in-depth look at the four critical Sandler questioning strategies, just as essential to the coach's information-gathering process as they are to the salesperson's. Effective coaches learn to use them to avoid falling into the surface-information trap.

Active Listening

Active listening is a fundamental information gathering tool used in coaching to help the coach dig deeper into the salesperson's issues and thus avoid potentially hazardous misconceptions and superficial understandings. Most sales managers listen with "one ear"—for a variety of reasons—and never fully engage with what the salesperson is saying. To put it bluntly, they're not present. Truth be told, this is true throughout the day, not just during coaching sessions. Such absence is dangerous. The manager may miss critical facts and respond based on incomplete information.

Skilled coaches pay full attention to the conversation—and the person—and utilize active listening. They sensitively restate thoughts the salesperson has communicated and offer some variation on the phrase, "Tell me more." Active listening is not just the monitoring of spoken words. Observation of body language and the tonality used allows the coach to better interpret the words used by the salesperson during the session to validate or challenge the salesperson's responses. Paraphrasing the responses given or even repeating specific phrases ensures a deeper understanding by both the coach and salesperson. Active listening is designed to help the coach truly hear everything before responding to something the salesperson says. This helps to ensure comprehension, eliminate misconceptions, and make unwarranted assumptions less likely.

Example

Salesperson: "I'm asking a lot of questions during my sales calls."

Manager: "That's great that you're asking questions. Can you tell me a little more about the types of questions you ask?"

Salesperson: "The questions in the Sandler Pain Funnel®."

Manager: "Okay—the Pain Funnel Questions. That's a good place to start. Could you do something for me?"

Salesperson: "Sure."

Manager: "Here's a sheet of paper and a pen. What I'd like you to do is take a moment to write down the specific questions in the Pain Funnel—and then write the typical responses you receive to each of those questions."

Salesperson: "Well. Maybe I don't ask all of them—but I definitely find pain."

The Dummy Curve

The Sandler questioning strategy known as the **Dummy Curve**, which we discussed earlier in the book is necessary to prevent the coach from fixing problems by telling the salesperson what to do. (In fact, telling the salesperson what to do hardly ever resolves the problems.) The Dummy Curve technique is based on the idea that the other person, either the prospect in a selling situation or the salesperson in a coaching situation, must do 70% of the talking during the session. The coach fills the remaining 30% with questions designed to get the salesperson to give critical information about the issue or problem, including questions that make the coach seem to not know as much as he does. When the salesperson is answering, the coach is gathering valuable information vital to the solution.

Example

Salesperson: "My up-front contract was solid. I mean, it was airtight."

Manager: "Got it. So what are the elements of your up-front contract?"

Salesperson: "Well, I cover time, the prospect's agenda, my agenda, and the outcome of the sales call."

Manager: "I may have missed it, but did you preview your biggest fear about the outcome of the meeting during your up-front contract?"

Salesperson: "No, I'm not comfortable reviewing that so I usually eliminate it."

Strip-Lining

Another Sandler questioning strategy helpful in keeping the focus on the salesperson is the **strip-lining** technique I've mentioned earlier in the book. This may involve a softening statement used to mitigate any harshness that may unintentionally be associated with questions asked by the coach or statements made by the salesperson. Think of strip-lining as what you do instead of contradicting the other person or trying to change the other person's opinion. Phrases like, "That's interesting," "I hear that a lot," "I'm not surprised," or "That sounds important," are designed to nurture the salesperson and create a safe environment where the salesperson is free to share personal information that goes below the surface of the problem. Applied correctly, strip-lining is needed to disarm the salesperson since it usually includes a 180-degree-opposite response to what the salesperson may be expecting.

Example

Salesperson: "I guess I'm just not comfortable asking how much money my prospect is losing when I'm probing pain."

Manager: "A lot of the salespeople I work with feel the same way. What if I were to tell you that monetary loss is the first step in creating value in the mind of your prospect?"

Salesperson: "I never thought of it that way. It makes sense."

Reversing

The last information-gathering strategy is called **reversing**. Using this extremely powerful tactic means responding to a question with a question in order to clarify its meaning or gather more information. It takes some practice because most people have a lifetime of conditioning to answer questions as soon as they are posed. Many coaches fail because they fall into the trap of giving a premature opinion or comment. This may derail the coaching session by focusing the answer on the coach's perspective instead of the salesperson's.

Example

Salesperson: "My prospects constantly tell me my price is too high and shop my proposals to the competition. What am I supposed to do?"

Manager: "Why do you think they do that?"

Salesperson: "Because low price is the most important thing. That is what they value. Right?"

Manager: "What do they tell you when you get to the bottom of the Pain Funnel and you ask how much the problem is costing them?"

Salesperson: "They usually say, 'A whole lot of money!'"

Manager: "What if you had them tell you a specific dollar loss instead of a vague answer like, 'A whole lot of money'?"

Salesperson: "Hmm. Well, in that case, they would have a specific figure to compare against price and possibly see I'm providing a fair price for my product."

Manager: "How could that help?"

Salesperson: "It would allow them to match the exact money they are losing against my price and show value."

SANDLER COACHING INSIGHT

Preparation counts! The Preparation checklist for an effective coach includes:

- Questions to ask to gather deeper information
- Questions to handle salesperson's objections
- Questions to help the salesperson change his mindset about key issues
- Questions to raise the salesperson's awareness of the issue
- Strip-lines and reverses that fit the coach's style
- Dummy Curve reverses to uncover the salesperson's true depth of knowledge

---

PREPARATION

Preparation is one of the keys to a productive coaching session. The effective coach prepares a questioning strategy in advance of the actual session and then spontaneously executes the plan during the session without seeming to be following a checklist. The goal is not to recite a list of to-do items, but to focus on raising the salesperson's awareness of the choices he faces in dealing with the problem at hand. A carefully prepared strategic questioning process, executed flexibly and incorporating constructive and challenge-driven feedback, provides the coach with the ability to listen with a nonjudgmental attitude. Such a process creates an atmosphere safe enough to explore the salesperson's deepest problems.

- **Constructive feedback** is specific, behavior-focused, non-judgmental commentary delivered in a nurturing fashion so the salesperson accepts it without feeling a personal attack. Thought-provoking feedback focuses on helping the salesperson think differently about a given strategy or tactic.
- **Challenge-driven feedback** is not a personal attack, either. It's designed to focus the salesperson on setting goals that stretch his thinking about a strategy currently being employed. The coach should never give feedback that places the salesperson in the position of being judged. This has a negative impact on self-worth.

Feedback from the coach is an extremely important part of the coaching session. It provides the salesperson with direction and additional guidance. Unfortunately, some feedback that can be viewed as criticism or judgment may actually end up having a negative impact on the salesperson's self-worth.

The best feedback is constructive. It's meant to provoke deeper thought or further conversation, and it allows the coach to offer suggestions for the salesperson to consider. It is extremely important to give feedback without adding praise or judgment to the information. Feedback must be based on the coach's observation or on hard, verifiable information the salesperson has actually provided during the session, rather than on anecdotes or the hollow accolades of wishful thinking. The salesperson must be able to connect the coach's feedback to reality. The feedback should be logical and be delivered in the context of the coaching issue.

Many coaches think they are passing along constructive feedback when they are in fact sending mixed messages. Consider a comment like this: "Sounds like you made a great sales call, but you need to work on helping the prospect determine the financial impact of the problem you uncovered." The use of the word "but" acts as a fact eraser. It removes the thought expressed prior to it and emphasizes the thought expressed after it. The coach should find an effective way to focus feedback on the real issue and avoid the hollow rhetoric about a "great sales call."

In order for feedback to be effective, it needs to be specific and avoid generalities. Many coaches who try to wing it during a session add a lot of fluffy comments that sound like compliments but don't connect to anything tangible. Usually, they are hoping the salesperson will receive a motivational lift. The problem is, these comments lack substance and cause confusion in the mind of the salesperson.

The Feedback Loop

Effective coaches utilize a methodology called the **feedback loop** to respond to the issues discussed during the coaching session. Sandler's feedback loop methodology provides a formal way to help the salesperson understand the thoughts conveyed by the coach. The feedback loop is simply a way to offer a coaching reaction to any issue discussed during the session. It differs from the seven-step coaching methodology in that it is flexible enough to be used to deal with nearly any immediate issue the salesperson faces, with little or no formal preparation ahead of time.

The feedback loop has five stages:

1. **Salesperson's assessment:** During this stage, the salesperson gives relevant information on the situation from his perspective. The salesperson should not filter any information as good or bad, but simply explain his version of the event. This stage involves gathering information on the salesperson's perspective on the situation and the relevant behavior.

2. **Coach's assessment:** After the salesperson gives his viewpoint, it's up to the coach to assess whether additional information is needed. Since the salesperson is continuously providing new information, the effective coach weighs all comments to decide what is pertinent to the session and what is superfluous. Active listening is extremely important in gathering the salesperson's perspective. The effective

coach listens with "both ears" and asks as many questions as necessary to understand the depth of the issue.

3. **Awareness gap analysis:** The coach now determines the salesperson's level of awareness and, if it is low, raises it by helping the salesperson recognize key information that may have been missed. Awareness is raised by focusing the salesperson's attention on all details influencing the outcome that the salesperson may have missed.

4. **Real-time understanding:** This stage is reached when the salesperson begins to draw conclusions that are different from his initial thinking. These new thoughts drive growth as well as buy-in to a different course of action. Skillful questioning helps the coach provide a fresh perspective on the issue.

5. **Ownership of feedback:** The salesperson's new way of thinking about the problem or situation helps him to adapt his behavior the next time the problem arises and breaks a habitual behavioral pattern that isn't working. This critical buy-in locks in the result and drives commitment to change.

The Feedback Loop is continuous with input/output.
Once the fifth step is completed, the process can
be repeated for continuous growth.

The feedback loop creates a dynamic learning process where understanding is derived from narrowing the gap between current thinking about a problem and a new perspective.

CARLOS'S STORY

Carlos is a sales veteran who has had a very successful sales career. He is constantly challenging himself to get to the next level and continuously raises his performance bar. Jim, Carlos's sales manager, feels Carlos should begin calling on large, enterprise-size accounts since this would raise his contribution to the company and add to Carlos's income. Carlos has been struggling with closing business and has been using the Sandler system the same way he did with his smaller accounts.

Salesperson's assessment: Carlos was confused about his lack of success. He felt he was using the Sandler system the same way he always had in the past. The system, according to Carlos, "just stopped working." Carlos debriefed each step of the system in his journal and gave himself high marks for execution.

Coach's assessment: Jim asked Carlos about the strength of the relationship he was forming with the prospects. He also questioned Carlos about his sales template, that is, the number of "touches" or meetings Carlos had with the prospect on the way to closing the business. Jim determined that Carlos was "rushing the sale"—because he, Carlos, felt he needed it to close sooner.

Jim then developed a template for Carlos to use in executing the Sandler system with larger accounts. Unlike the template for accounts with a single decision maker, this template had seven steps and took forty-five days to execute. These seven steps required a series of meetings where the prospect gained comfort with Carlos and exchanged information at a slower pace.

The first step in the template was solely designed to build the relationship; the second step was designed to build a roadmap including a timeline for actions both parties would take; the third step involved determining the pain; the fourth step involved exploring budget and the prospect's decision process. The presentation and product demo took place in the fifth step, after about thirty days and three meetings. Carlos would negotiate value and onboard the new client in the next two steps.

Awareness gap analysis: Jim's questioning about the template for enterprise accounts helped Carlos realize that although he had been using the Sandler system, he was used to smaller accounts who reacted faster. Since these smaller accounts didn't have the layer of leadership that larger accounts had and the size of the sales was smaller, the sales cycle was shorter.

Real-time understanding: Carlos realized he had to slow down and spend more time developing the relationship and set an up-front contract with a clear timeline and steps to be executed over a longer timeframe. This provided a roadmap for both Carlos and the prospect to follow during the longer enterprise sales cycle.

Ownership of feedback: Carlos decided he would build a timeline for each prospect and share it with Jim at the beginning of the sales process. He would map the seven steps in Jim's template and put dates next to each step to create a pace for closing the business. Jim committed to review this chart weekly to uncover any flaws in Carlos's execution of the process. Carlos slowed down his execution of the Sandler system and found it made him more effective in his new role.

Jim's skillful use of the coaching feedback loop helped Carlos see problems he had missed and make corrections to prevent future problems.

STRATEGIC THINKING

Strategic thinking is one of the most valuable tools in the coach's toolbox. It is driven by curiosity. The effective coach is able to draw a wide circle around any coaching situation and analyze all the factors contributing to the salesperson's situation. The ability to think strategically helps the coach avoid the temptation to narrow the coaching process too quickly and turn it into a problem-solving session.

Curiosity is a wonderful attribute for a coach to develop since it drives continuous learning. Similar coaching situations present themselves in a variety of ways; each salesperson has a different perspective on the salient problems. This is why the effective coach cannot apply "off the rack" solutions, choosing instead to customize an approach that will fit the salesperson's situation and personality. The coach develops a unique understanding of the salesperson by questioning his own beliefs about the information the salesperson is providing. This eliminates a "one size fits all" mentality and helps the coach remember that all salespeople are different—even when they bring similar-sounding problems to the coaching sessions.

Successful coaches re-energize their coaching process by continuously challenging themselves to grow. They test their own thinking as well as their perspective and focus on helping the salesperson discover the answers—instead of reciting them.

Four important elements an effective coach incorporates into his strategic thinking process in order to be more effective are listed below.

Challenge

The effective coach challenges the thinking of the salesperson as well as his own thoughts about the situation. This eliminates "if...then" formulaic problem solving: "If the salesperson says this, then the coach says that." Even if the end result is familiar, the process of arriving at that point still has to challenge the thinking of both parties.

Broaden

The effective coach widens each coaching situation to its broadest point by asking exploratory questions designed to touch upon even the fringe areas of the issue in question. It is dangerous to narrow the coaching situation too quickly since the coach may miss important outlier issues critical to the eventual solution. This process of broadening can create a mind map of the issues impacting the problem—a visual way of organizing the thoughts the salesperson is expressing. One easy way to develop a mind map is to write the coaching issue in the center of a blank sheet of paper and draw a circle around it. Next, think of all the macro issues affecting the issue and place each one on a line emanating from the circle. These lines represent the big picture thoughts, goals, strategies, problems, etc., affecting the problem in the circle. Lastly, from the large macro lines, draw micro lines to define the details affecting the macro issues. This process broadens the issue and creates a map that is used to explore all the ancillary impact issues so none are missed.

Mind Map
Prospecting Example

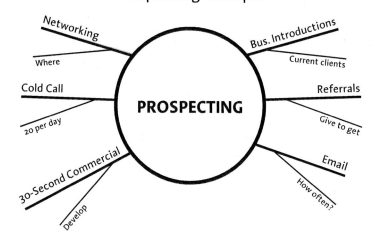

Deepen

The effective coach probes below the surface of the issue to discover any potential "iceberg effects." The captain of the Titanic learned an important fact about icebergs during his maiden voyage—ninety percent of an iceberg is below the surface. This sometimes makes a sea voyage interesting. So it is for coaching problems. Ninety percent of the information necessary to help the salesperson attain greater success is below the surface. That information must be explored strategically in order to achieve the coaching goal. The coach can use a process similar to the Sandler Pain Funnel, which offers a sequence of questions salespeople can ask, to explore the issues contributing to the salesperson's problem.

A similar funnel can be used with the salesperson during a coaching session.

THE SANDLER COACHING FUNNEL

1. What are you trying to accomplish? What is the goal or problem resolution?
2. What is driving this goal or problem resolution?
3. What actions have you taken so far?
4. What roadblocks do you have to overcome?
5. What is your level of motivation to change?
6. What's holding you back from achieving the goal or solving the problem?
7. What is your level of commitment to success?
8. How do you benefit from accomplishing the goal or solving the problem?
9. What meaningful action can you take at this time to make progress?
10. How can I [the coach] help you achieve the goal or solve the problem?

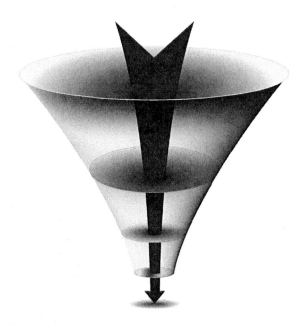

Such a process moves the salesperson from intellectual discussion to emotional engagement, which is essential to making a rational decision to change.

Just as the Pain Funnel moves a prospect, the Coaching Funnel moves the salesperson through three distinct areas to reach the final conclusion: big-picture exploration of the problem or goal; the reason the goal must be achieved or problem solved; and a positive outcome for the salesperson.

10% Above the surface

Intellectual Feedback

Emotional Engagement

ANGER

FEAR

HAPPINESS

DOUBT

UNCERTAINTY

90% Below the surface

PRIDE

Learn

The effective coach continuously learns new approaches to address all the issues salespeople bring to the table. Stagnant coaches lose impact, and their effectiveness dwindles over time. Many sales forces stop growing because salespeople realize they are receiving recycled messages in their coaching sessions. The salespeople stop requesting coaching, and their behavior begins to deteriorate. Coaches should continuously look for ineffective coaching patterns and refresh specific knowledge of the characteristics, behavior, beliefs, and skills of their salespeople. Use of the Devine Inventory and Extended DISC assessments helps coaches analyze the opportunities and strengths of specific salespeople and may even uncover themes holding entire sales teams back. Additionally, effective coaches are always on the lookout for new ways to deliver coaching messages to their salespeople so the salespeople learn to expect fresh ideas and approaches that will inspire them.

THE ROLE OF JOURNALING

Journaling is a powerful tool that helps the coach build a trajectory for the salesperson to track progress. Many coaches and salespeople shy away from using it. They see journaling as a kind of juvenile, "dear diary" approach to reporting on their day instead of what it is: an engaging way of measuring personal growth. Journaling is used to analyze periods of high performance, as well as those times when performance has dipped below acceptable levels and the salesperson needs to determine why. Keeping a journal doesn't have to be a complex, time-consuming act. The goal of journaling is for salespeople to record thoughts and feelings as well as goals, aspirations, and behavioral commitments each day, prior to beginning work, and then review accomplishments at the end of their day. Bookending each day with journaling helps salespeople see successes, roadblocks, ineffective patterns, blind spots, and growth opportunities. The journaling process helps the salesperson, of course, but it also helps the coach understand the relationship between thought and action. Salespeople who begin their day with goals and a positive feeling about the day tend to perform at a higher level than those who have strong negative feelings at the start. Once the relevant feelings are recorded, the coach can help the salesperson overcome negative thoughts by recommending and reinforcing consistent, positive behaviors that can be performed over a 20-day period. Without such a response to negative behavior-belief patterns, the salesperson may blame his lack of success on external factors.

The coach typically reviews the journal with the salesperson after twenty days of the salesperson's executing the activity. The 20-day review is important as it removes performance spikes, both high and low, and helps both coach and salesperson focus on the pattern of behavior creating the belief system. Reviewing the journal daily is not effective. It tends to focus on performance as an event instead of a pattern. Skills, knowledge, and application patterns become visible to the salesperson only over time.

Here is a process for effective journaling.

- The salesperson commits to keeping a journal during the entire coaching process.

- The journal should have entries in the morning before the start of the workday and in the evening prior to the end of the salesperson's workday.

- The morning page consists of feelings at the start of the day and personal and professional goals for the day. These goals are designed to drive behavior that improves the salesperson's professional success and strengthens his inner beliefs.

- The journal process should continue for twenty straight days without stopping and should be reviewed by the coach on the twenty-first day. This review by the coach and salesperson determines relevant streams of consciousness (important topics that keep recurring in the journal) as well as behavioral patterns that are important to understand. You'll learn more about streams of consciousness in Chapter Ten.

- The coach helps the salesperson set goals to overcome problems caused by habitually unproductive behavior or beliefs.

- The coach, in turn, keeps a similar journal about the salesperson to record progress, and this is reviewed with the salesperson every ninety days.

Coaches should also keep a private journal on each of the salespeople they coach. This journal helps coaches be more effective since they can refer to it from time to time to discover patterns of behavior or beliefs specific to the individual they are coaching. To save time, the coach should review this journal prior to each coaching session to get up to speed on the salesperson's history. The journal should include comments from the salesperson's Devine Inventory and Extended DISC assessments, observations from past sessions, and notes on effective approaches to specific problems or issues, patterns, and beliefs.

USE THE TOOLBOX

When combined with the seven-step Sandler Coaching System, the toolbox I've outlined in this chapter helps the coach raise the level of coaching from a simple motivational conversation to an effective process designed to help the salesperson grow. The time invested in coaching should be focused on developing sustainable success and a positive outcome, rather than on hollow inspirational sayings. Remember: Your toolbox should be customized to fit your personality, and used regularly, in order for you to continuously raise effectiveness.

SANDLER COACHING RULES

- Practice all questioning strategies prior to each session and make them a natural part of the coaching methodology.
- Give constructive feedback that allows you to help the salesperson understand actions at a deeper level and accept your perspective on the need for change.

- Use strategic thinking to broaden the salesperson's problem to encompass fringe areas that may be important to the solution.

- Work with the salesperson to develop the skill of journaling as a roadmap to greater success.

- Customize your coaching toolbox to fit your personality, and practice regularly in order to continuously increase its effectiveness.

CHAPTER NINE

Thoughts Influence Performance

OVERVIEW

- Thought control
- The sales "yips"
- Creative visualization
- Training the brain to win

In this chapter, you will learn how and why negative thoughts tend to limit performance, while positive thoughts tend to drive greater success.

THOUGHT CONTROL

> *Your beliefs become your thoughts.*
> *Your thoughts become your words.*
> *Your words become your actions.*
> *Your actions become your habits.*
> *Your habits become your values.*
> *Your values become your destiny.*
>
> —*Mahatma Gandhi*

Many salespeople, as we have seen, develop limiting behavior patterns. Often, these are driven by the subconscious thoughts they have developed over the course of their careers. Subconscious thought patterns are often derived from negative or positive past selling experiences. These patterns can build up over time to create behavior blockages.

These mental roadblocks are a little bit like savings bonds—they mature over time. Instead of receding with the passage of time, as you might expect, they can have a bigger and bigger impact. There's an old saying, and a wise one: "Be careful what you think." It's deeply relevant to both salespeople and to coaches since thoughts tend to influence actions. Higher-performing salespeople and coaches harness the power of behavior to influence thought.

NADIR'S STORY

Nadir has been a client of mine for fifteen years. He began attending a morning Sandler sales training program called

Foundations in 2000, and his use of the Sandler system had an immediate and positive impact on his performance. Nadir raised his closing percentage and made more money than he had ever dreamed of making; his lifestyle improved dramatically over the next few years.

Nadir's success stalled in 2003, though. Early in that year, he began to slip back into his old patterns, in spite of the training and support he was receiving. This downward spiral caused Nadir's sales manager Gabriela to spend more and more time coaching him, even giving him special one-on-one training sessions—all to no avail. Something was wrong, but no one knew what. Nadir asked if I would work with him one-on-one, and I agreed.

Nadir had the skills he needed to succeed, but after a few sessions it became clear to me that his limiting behavior patterns, rooted in difficult past experiences, were re-emerging (they do that!) and subconsciously sabotaging his success.

Nadir's problem had taken root many years before. He grew up on a farm and spent many hours listening to his father's thoughts about the world as they worked together in the fields. One of his father's favorite topics was money and the impact it had on the wealthy segment of the population. He believed wealthy people had questionable values and sacrificed their ethics in order to be successful. He cautioned Nadir to avoid the pitfalls associated with accumulating wealth.

As Nadir became more successful, he began to raise his income level. Although he never considered himself wealthy, he came to feel uncomfortable with living in a bigger house in an affluent neighborhood. Nadir's thoughts about his current financial position triggered old beliefs, and he began to limit his own success—subconsciously!—so that he wouldn't fall into the trap described by his father. The more money Nadir made, the more his feelings about money negatively impacted his behavior and caused his performance to plateau.

I also coached Nadir's manager Gabriela. I wanted to help her understand Nadir's need to work toward something greater than money.

Gabriela discovered that Nadir's mother had died of breast cancer five years earlier. One of Nadir's responses to this tragedy had been a growing desire to do something to fight the terrible disease that had taken her out of his life forever. Gabriela encouraged Nadir to meet with members of an association focused on helping women dealing with breast cancer to maintain hope as they went through chemotherapy. Nadir began contributing money and time to this cause and soon found a number of ways to use his financial resources to support what really mattered to him. Nadir also began working with the Special Olympics, inspired by a family member who was disabled.

Nadir's money issues didn't disappear overnight, but he did find a way to deal with them in a positive way and release a limiting belief—"wealthy people are immoral"—that was holding him hostage.

Once we were able to deal with this internal "recording," Nadir was able to perform at his best once again, and he resumed his position as the top performer on his sales team.

THE INTERNAL RECORDING

Internal recordings such as "wealthy people are immoral" can play in the background (or foreground) of a person's mind for decades. They are extremely difficult to overcome, and multiple sessions (along with therapy, possibly) are necessary for the coach and the salesperson to get to the root causes.

Coaches are not therapists, of course, but they can help salespeople deal with hidden, subconscious enemies—and they can play the role of detective. Ideally, both participants are detectives. Together, the salesperson and the coach can discover the reason the salesperson thinks as he does about certain subjects.

These subconscious thought patterns are subtle and quite powerful. They usually define the way a salesperson will act when faced with the situation triggering the limiting belief, just as Nadir's belief that wealth was immoral was triggered by his first real experience of financial success.

OVERCOMING THE YIPS

An online encyclopedia defines *the yips* as "the loss of fine motor skills without apparent explanation, in one of a number of different sports." The entry goes on to explain that athletes affected by

SANDLER COACHING INSIGHT

High performers typically control their thought patterns, while lower performers are typically controlled by the way they think. Coaches can ask salespeople the following seven questions in order to get them to identify, unlock, and overcome unproductive thoughts and beliefs.

1. Why do you think that way?
2. If the opposite thought were true, would you act differently?
3. What is the benefit to you from this new action?
4. What's the worst thing that can happen when you take this action?
5. What's the best thing that could possibly happen?
6. How would the best outcome impact your results?
7. Can you live with the result if the worst happens?

Long-standing thoughts and beliefs typically create strong emotions and opinions that go untested. These seven questions can help free the salesperson to think more broadly about a problem and explore new approaches to recurring issues.

this mysterious disorder demonstrate a "sudden, unexplained loss of previous skills." Those affected may recover their abilities, may change technique in order to compensate, or may "abandon their sport at the highest level." The term is said to have been popularized by Tommy Armour, a great golf champion of the 1920s and '30s, to explain the putting difficulties that led him to abandon tournament play.

Salespeople can also fall prey to the yips. When a salesperson gets the yips, he knows what he should do during the sales call, but he simply can't execute it.

Over the years, I've seen a lot of cases of the yips in salespeople. The disorder usually begins when the salesperson starts listening to internal negative self-talk and develops a mentality best described as, "Let's get this call over with since it's not going to end well." Many sales managers write this off as a skill-set issue. They offer training as a solution, but find it doesn't work. Other coaches assume the problem is lack of practice, but it is so much deeper than that.

In golf, the yips arise when the muscles are not aligned with the brain. In sales, they show up when the selling strategies are not in sync with the belief system prevailing in the subconscious mind.

WHAT DO YOU SAY TO YOURSELF?

Shad Helmstetter, PhD, the best-selling author of *What Do You Say When You Talk to Yourself*, tells us that as much as 70% of our thoughts are negative enough to create fear in our minds. This fear develops negative mental images that become locked in the subconscious mind. Such images, Helmstetter writes, not only build patterns of behavior, but also create a physiological response. Bottom line: When you think thoughts that create fearful pictures, you put your body under pressure.

AMY'S STORY

Amy was a new salesperson who works for one of my clients. Since she was only hired recently and currently had very few clients, her days were filled with cold calling to find prospects to qualify for sales calls. Cold calling means hearing a whole lot of *no* answers, so it takes persistence and strong self-worth to make any personal cold-calling campaign effective.

Amy had attended numerous Sandler training sessions to learn the mechanics of successful cold calling. She understood the technique. Once she was actually on the phone, though, she struggled. Aggressive personalities were the most difficult for her to handle on the phone. Her mind filled with negative thoughts in the critical seconds before a prospect answered the phone. By the time she said, "Hello," Amy had already built a mental state that put her at a distinct disadvantage. She anticipated the call ending badly—and, as expected, it did. She repeated this process fifty to sixty times a day, getting more discouraged with each dial.

Amy's sales manager Bob told me that he shadowed her phone calls weekly and gave her plenty of advice on her 30-second commercial, her pain indicator questions, her tonality, and even her body language. Nothing seemed to make any difference. A few weeks before, Amy accepted Bob's coaching in an attempt to improve, and diligently prepared for each call. Her spirits were high and she appeared to be fully committed to a positive outcome. But once she started dialing, she encountered the same negative result. Now it seemed that Bob's advice only made matters worse.

Bob asked me if I could help. I agreed to interview Amy and follow the same path Bob took, shadowing her actual phone calls. I found that Amy's preparation was flawless. She followed my 5-5-5 phone methodology: five minutes to prepare, five minutes for the call, and five minutes to debrief the result. I determined quickly that the problem was not with her external technique or the delivery of her message. It was Amy's internal mindset that sabotaged the result. Mentally, she expected to fail. She created a belief system of doubt, fear, and anxiety, which, in turn, drove failure on each call.

Amy's fear created a mental block that she had to overcome before any of the techniques she was applying could work. As her failures began to mount, she started to doubt not only herself, but her desire to have a sales career.

I noticed that Amy was using a traditional opening: "Is this a good time to speak?" and hoping the answer would be, "Yes." Her mind began to spiral downward whenever the answer was, "No." It occurred to me that the dynamic of the call might change if Amy heard the word "yes" early on in the call. I asked her to change the opening to, "Have I caught you at a bad time?" When the response was "Yes"—which it often was—she followed up with, "I thought it might be. Busy executives rarely have time for my phone calls." This seemingly minor change in the first few seconds of the discussion changed her outlook and began to eliminate her fears early. She found it much easier to maintain composure for the remainder of the call.

I worked with Bob and helped him utilize creative visualization during coaching sessions in order to help Amy see her problem as well as attain a better result from her calling efforts. In just twenty days, Amy was showing greater comfort and success on the phone. She felt renewed confidence in her choice to pursue sales as a career.

CREATIVE VISUALIZATION

Creative visualization harnesses the power of the imagination and turns it into positive thinking. This technique involves seeing desirable events or situations in a positive light over and over again, until the memory of the event becomes real in one's mind.

Athletes have been using creative visualization for a long time to see positive outcomes in their sport performance. I have known professional basketball players who stand at the foul line shooting imaginary foul shots and seeing the ball go in the basket each time. I have met professional golfers who practice six-foot putts using the visualization of the ball dropping in the cup. In each case, the mind is focused on a positive result, over and over again, and begins to accept the outcome as reality.

For my part, I am an average golfer. For the longest time, I struggled with my driver. Chris, my golf coach, began working with me on visualization techniques about two years ago. It was the best thing that ever happened to my golf game. I developed a pre-shot routine in the tee box using visualization. It helps me make sure my grip is correct, my feet are set in the correct position, and my posture is aligned prior to my swing. Additionally, I stand six feet behind the teed up golf ball and look down the fairway to find my ideal landing spot for the drive. I stare at it until I develop comfort. I stay in this position until I have a mental image locked in place and am confident I can execute a drive to hit that spot. Once I feel my subconscious mind has accepted this idea, I return to the ball and go through the grip, feet, and posture mechanics allowing me to have the proper form.

The bottom line: My driving accuracy has improved by an astonishing 70%. Inspired by this positive change, I have since adopted a "pre-shot routine" for sales calls utilizing the Sandler selling methodology.

AMY'S STORY (CONTINUED)

I asked Amy to imagine and write down a detailed description of a prospecting phone call resulting in a positive conversation with the prospect. In this written description, Amy made it clear that she delivered her phone call with perfect body language and tonality, using a solid 30-second commercial and three pain-indicating questions that made her prospect want to speak with her more. At the end of the conversation, the prospect agreed to meet with Amy in person and explore the potential of doing business together.

As Amy read aloud her perfect scenario, her face lit up. A

broad smile expressed her comfort with the situation. Once she was done reading, I asked her to close her eyes and focus on the situation she had just described. She repeated the situation out loud three times in her own words with her eyes closed. Then I asked her a series of questions regarding her experience. Here's what I asked her:

- "What do you see around you as a result of this positive experience?" (I had Amy carefully describe in visual terms all that she was witnessing with her mind's eye.)
- "What do you hear people saying about you as a result of this positive experience?" (I had her listen carefully to the voices commenting on her success.)
- "What do you feel deep inside as a result of the success you are achieving from this positive experience?" (With this question, Amy accessed all the positive emotions and unleashed those feelings so she could experience the joy associated with her success.)

I worked with Amy and her sales manager to arrange a schedule where Amy could make fewer cold calls daily for the next five days. This would allow her some extra time to utilize the visualization process five times during the course of those five days. We tracked the results. Even though Amy struggled during the first two days of the new exercise (just as I had on the golf course), she showed definite improvement by the end of the week. Prior to this, Amy typically had three conversations and made no appointments with prospects during her 50- to 60-dial day. After utilizing this process, Amy had fifteen conversations and scheduled three qualified appointments.

This dramatic change came about solely as a result of simply visualizing a different outcome. As Amy worked on her visualization process for the next twenty days, she created a new positive experience and turned it into a new productive habit.

Creative visualization unlocks the mind and frees it to think about new desired states. "If you can think it, you can achieve it" is a mantra the effective coach utilizes to help salespeople grow past self-imposed limitations.

TRAINING THE BRAIN TO WIN

Winners think and act differently than the rest of the world. Their winning is a habit driven by their behavior—not the other way around. A winner's mentality is fueled by the "need versus want" model.

Understanding the mental difference between needs and wants is critical to helping the salesperson. *Need* implies commitment, while *want* focuses on desire. Someone may want to join a health club to get in better physical shape, but not take action. The need to join the health club after a doctor recommends doing so is based on a dire, non-negotiable health issue. The effective coach constantly challenges salespeople to express new, meaningful "need" goals in order to keep them reaching beyond their grasp.

The mind learns about winning at an early age when a child

begins to compete in sports or in academic activities. Children are celebrated when they win and embarrassed when they lose. These feelings either further trigger the need to win consistently or create a withdrawal from activities evoking these feelings. The effective coach identifies these adjustments and helps the salesperson learn the best ways to deal with them.

Successful athletes spend a lot of time building mental toughness to support their physical attributes. Salespeople can mirror this process to develop successful sales careers. Coaches must work with them to build the same mental toughness, systematically building both confidence and a laser-like focus on success. This helps the salesperson as well as the athlete move into the "higher gear" necessary for consistent superior performance.

Athletic coaches follow a performance improvement model involving the proper mix of practice, game-day behavior execution, and "skull sessions" that include film review and game-day observation. Training the salesperson's brain to win consistently requires the sales coach to establish a similar process. This necessitates the coach developing a routine involving regular role-play practice sessions, sales call briefing and debriefing activities, sales call observation, and consistent coaching sessions to build mental toughness.

As part of this process, salespeople must set short-term goals, accomplished daily, to help build a success track. These goals begin to stretch their ability, challenge the status quo, and eliminate complacency. Goals such as "one more sales call per week," "one more productive phone conversation from a cold-calling session,"

or "one more challenging question during a sales call" can significantly influence the salesperson's productivity over the course of a
year. The coach must continuously analyze the sales force to find
growth challenges and eliminate mediocrity and complacency.
You may have heard the phrase, "Practice makes perfect."
Actually, this saying is only half true. Superior athletes and consistently high-performing salespeople should adjust the phrase to
read, "Perfect practice makes perfect."

Practice in the salesperson's world means role-play. Perfect
practice means role-play in real world situations with a "gloves
off" approach from the person in the role of the prospect, as if
the situation were real. The role-play must be thoroughly executed
in real time, with no time outs, and then debriefed by the coach.
These real-life conditions allow the salesperson to test new strategies and tactics in a safe environment as well as improve by turning
mistakes into points of learning on the way to success. Lower-
performing salespeople either avoid role-play activities altogether
or bluff their way through the exercise, never fully benefitting
from the power that goes with perfect practice.

It's particularly important that the salesperson use the coach to
debrief on the behavior executed in all key sales calls (not just on
the role-plays). Ideally, the coach should accompany the salesperson on sales calls from time to time to make observations and look
for patterns and blind spots. This continual debriefing provides
the coach with insights on a behavioral profile the salesperson
might otherwise never realize exists.

Real-life sales calls add the element of pressure so the coach can witness the influence that it has on the salesperson's performance. The pressure created by the buyer-seller interaction can significantly influence the outcome of the sales call—in either direction—so the coach must observe this firsthand.

THINKING MATTERS

There is a definite link between the way salespeople think and the effect those thoughts have on their actions, and thus on performance. Salespeople must control their thoughts so they don't subconsciously sabotage their own success.

SANDLER COACHING RULES

- Make sure negative thoughts don't limit the ability to execute productive behavior.
- Help salespeople recognize negative self-talk in its early stages and eliminate it.
- Use creative visualization to help salespeople see the future and then adopt behavior to achieve it.
- Build mental toughness to help salespeople support the behavior that must be executed in a sales call.
- Develop a training process similar to the process professional athletes use.

CHAPTER TEN

Becoming a High-Performance Coach

OVERVIEW

- Developing a guidance system
- Raising performance standards
- Commitment to ongoing learning
- Walking the tightrope

I n this chapter, you will learn about the four traits all high-performance sales coaches share and the ways these traits affect coaching success. Effective coaches are in a state of continuous learning about their own process, as well as about the salespeople they encounter. These coaches regularly upgrade their knowledge and raise their personal performance bar, just as they advise the salespeople they coach to do.

DEVELOPING A GUIDANCE SYSTEM

The effective coach builds a coaching framework and style specific to the personality of the salesperson. Coaching, as discussed earlier in this book, is not a "one size fits all" discipline. Each session must be customized in order to be effective. Assessing the needs of the salesperson is a critical goal for the coach, and this takes time. Some needs will be obvious immediately; others will only become apparent gradually. Each salesperson requires a guidance system that shows his unique pathway on the roadmap to success.

Almost every new car or phone now has a built-in global positioning system (GPS) that provides directions to any destination you are likely to want to reach. Even the most directionally challenged traveler can reach the correct address with minimal stress. This electronic map is detailed. It includes turn-by-turn directions as well as an overview of the territory so as to give perspective whenever it's needed.

Those who grew up without this technology know what a big deal it is. Sometimes travelers spent a whole lot of time getting lost, pulling over, unfolding paper maps, and trying to remember directions in the dark. The GPS makes all those problems a thing of the past. The traveler is never lost as long as the guidance system is active—but the traveler must remember to use it.

Coaches provide the same kind of "you're never lost" comfort—as long as the salesperson consistently involves them and uses the Sandler coaching model for the step-by-step guidance necessary to support the goal of modifying the salesperson's behavior.

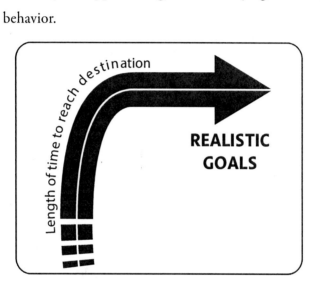

Coaching GPS:
• Setting realistic goals
• Timeframe to accomplish
• Establish communication style
• Application of the Sandler Coaching System

There are four keys to building a successful guidance system for a salesperson:

1. Analyzing the strength of the relationship between the coach and salesperson.

2. Setting realistic coaching goals, including the timeframe for accomplishing them.

3. Establishing a communication style that fits the salesperson's personality.

4. Applying the Sandler coaching methodology within the context of the selling situation.

KAYLA'S STORY

Kayla is a 10-year sales veteran who has a history of being a top performer in her company. She had a sales slump, though, when four of her largest customers had to deal with major market changes that led to dramatically reduced sales volume. Two of these clients were sold, forcing Kayla to establish new relationships. She lost one client to a competitor who presented a stronger business case. The final one faced a major lawsuit that led buying patterns to become much more conservative.

All of this had a major negative impact on Kayla's sales volume. Unfortunately, she had stopped prospecting for new business some months back and was relying on her four most valued customers, plus a few smaller customers, to deliver her sales quota. Not only was she now below her target, her prospecting skills had atrophied. She developed a severe case of call reluctance, driven by a deep discomfort with the whole idea of having to cold call again.

Meredith, her sales manager, was fearful of losing a valuable contributor like Kayla. She initiated the Sandler coaching process to help Kayla recover from this potentially devastating situation. Meredith assessed the relationship she had with Kayla and realized there was a lot of mistrust due to past experiences they had with one another. Her first step involved a candid conversation designed to knock down any barriers that might prevent them from being honest with each other during the coaching process. She used the Three P's of Trust process shared in Chapter Five and the Sandler coaching contract as a framework for their discussions. It took some candid conversations for both of them to become comfortable.

Once trust was firmly established, Meredith and Kayla mutually identified the large goal Kayla was committed to achieving: a healthy customer pool that connected to a specific numerical target. They then developed a series of small prospecting goals to feed the success of the large one. The small prospecting goals focused on networking different business associations in the area, using Kayla's current customers to gain business referrals, and conducting weekly business introduction meetings in which her larger customers could introduce her to other possible customers over testimonial lunches.

Since Kayla was an extremely direct communicator, a high "D" in Extended DISC terms, she always said exactly what was on her mind. She and Meredith agreed to be candid with each other and confront Kayla's issues head on.

Lastly, they detailed the Sandler Coaching System on a whiteboard and built a timeline for the process.

It took ninety days of renewed effort for Kayla to positively affect the problem she faced. During this time, she created a new sales Cookbook for Success, one heavily focused on prospecting for new business while reestablishing relationships with the new owners of the customers who were sold. With Meredith's coaching, Kayla modified her behavior model. Meredith helped her to develop greater comfort with her new plan. Kayla soon returned to her former status as a top performer—and learned how to make sure she never again fell into the trap of overreliance on existing customers to deliver her sales volume.

Meredith's skillful implementation of the Sandler coaching methodology helped Kayla use her GPS more effectively and recover from her sales slump. Having a clear map to move from point to point during the application of her new prospecting behaviors gave Kayla comfort and confidence that she could accomplish her goal—by following the road to her selling destination.

RAISING PERFORMANCE STANDARDS

In order for sales coaching to be effective, it must be applied to the individual behavior pattern of each salesperson so the coach can build a personalized developmental strategy that links learning to behavioral change. This personalized approach helps the coach work with the three performance levels inherent in every sales team: high, variable, and low. Of course, a salesperson's ability to improve performance is based on the choices he makes. The coach must develop the ability to work with each salesperson individually to encourage better behavioral choices and, in doing so, raise performance.

It is important for the coach to set a performance bar that can be used to measure acceptable behavior and sales results. The low and medium performers must commit to performance improvement, development, and growth so even lower performance comes in at levels that are acceptable in the eyes of company leaders. This performance bar must be established by setting behavioral metrics necessary for success. Here are some examples of the behavioral metrics I use to create a performance bar for a sales team.

Behavioral Metrics

1. **Number of "suspects" at the start of each week.** Salespeople should have an agreed-upon number of suspects (simply, an unqualified prospect) in their pipeline at the beginning of the week—that is, individuals who have shown initial interest in discussing the product or service without already having a relationship (bonding and rapport) or developed an agenda with an agreed-upon outcome (up-front contract). By Friday of each week, a salesperson should report on the number of sales calls already scheduled for the following week with suspects. Once the salesperson can qualify the strength of the relationship and has verified the person's agenda and commitment to a mutually beneficial outcome, the suspect becomes a prospect.

2. **First face-to-face appointments.** Each week, the salesperson should have a specific number of first in-person meetings

with prospects. Each industry has an optimal number. In some industries, the salesperson must have 6–8 first in-person meetings each week in order to meet sales goals.

3. **Active qualified proposals.** Each week, the salesperson should have a specific number of qualified proposals delivered after executing the Sandler selling process. A qualified proposal is one that has been derived from using the first five steps of the Sandler Selling System, thereby reaching the Fulfillment Step.

4. **Number of "close the sale" meetings.** Each week, the salesperson should have a specific number of meetings set up to close prospects who have been delivered proposals. The salesperson should be using the Sandler Selling System methodology to move sales from infancy to close, allowing the manager to debrief on the outcome, whether positive or negative. These "close the sale" meetings either result in a contract to business or the salesperson closing the file and not chasing ghosts.

5. **Number of prospecting hours.** Each week, salespeople should have executed a specific number of hours dedicated to prospecting. Sixty percent of the space on a salesperson's calendar should be dedicated to hunting for new business sources and 40% to nurturing existing customers for additional sales.

Weekly, and sometimes even daily, behavioral performance tracking can help the coach deal effectively with small issues connected to these targets before they become chronic problems. This form of behavior tracking becomes a smoke detector for the coach and can be used to create a kind of dashboard providing real-time behavior analytics. Such a dashboard helps the coach guide the salesperson in the present, when guidance counts, instead of after the fact.

COMMITMENT TO ONGOING LEARNING

By now, I hope you agree with me that coaching is not a static event. Rather, it is an ever-evolving practice of growth and professional development. Effective coaches continue to learn all they can about their salespeople and develop meaningful ways to empower them to advance their learning about their profession. The effective coach also continues to develop knowledge about the nature of salespeople, about buyer-seller interactions, about the Sandler system, and about new ways to trigger self-motivation for higher performance. Last but not least, effective coaches keep an eye out for new coaching strategies to help salespeople move to the next level of success.

Let's examine some of the more important continuous-learning areas for the effective coach in depth.

The Nature of Salespeople

Buried deep in the nature of every high-performing salesperson is the continuous need to sell the product or service to a prospect. This driving force must be harnessed and constructively channeled by the coach. Left alone, it creates many traps for the salesperson. Buyers love to encounter overly enthusiastic salespeople since they are able to exploit the blind spots many salespeople develop. Effective coaches raise their salespeople's awareness by balancing enthusiasm with reality. They help salespeople understand the importance of strategy in the sales profession and help them fight the urge to focus on "magical" (that is, hope-driven) tactics to close the sale.

The Buyer-Seller Interaction

Today's buyer acts much the same as buyers in the past did—with one notable exception. The Internet has made today's buyers far more informed, given them far more options, and left them far better prepared to deal with salespeople who use outdated traditional tactics to close sales. The effective coach understands the systematic approach today's buyers use in their attempts to control the sales call. At Sandler Training, we refer to this control as the "prospect's system." It begins with the buyer misleading the salesperson by feigning interest. From this step, the system moves forward to a request for a proposal, and evolves into a false negotiating process where the salesperson is forced to lower the price, sacrifice margin, and make general concessions to entice the buyer to act. In the final stage, the buyer, having negotiated multiple proposals from several sources, no longer has a need for the losing salesperson, avoids all contact, and moves on. The salesperson, however, still believing he has a chance to close the deal, continues the chase hoping for one last closing conversation. The coach is responsible for helping the salesperson understand the power of the prospect's system, the various ways today's communication technologies strengthen the prospect's hand, and the best ways to avoid letting the prospect "lead the dance."

The Sandler Selling System Methodology

The Sandler sales process has an element of science, making it systematic, and an element of art, making it fluid and customized for each selling situation. The science of the Sandler Selling System methodology lies in the systematic use of a clear selling process: the Sandler Submarine, which creates a very different dynamic than the prospect's system, as well as the Success Triangle, which focuses on behavior, attitude, and technique. The effective coach helps the salesperson improve in each critical point of the triangle without converting the coaching session into a one-on-one training session. The art of the Sandler Selling System methodology lies in the coach helping the salesperson personalize each compartment of the submarine so that it does the job it's designed to do and conforms to the characteristics and attributes of the individual buyer and the selling situation.

Motivation

The coach is responsible for helping the salesperson develop internal motivation. This is the only true form of motivation that sustains growth. Coaches who rely on external "rah rah" forms of motivation may experience a short-term blip in results, but they inevitably find that the salesperson falls back into old patterns. Internal motivation is developed when the coach helps the salesperson set meaningful goals to improve self-worth as well as professional status. As we have seen, motivation from within provides the fuel necessary for salespeople to continuously work on themselves when they are away from the actual coaching session, ensuring that the salesperson takes personal responsibility for growth. No coach ever learns all there is to learn about internal motivation. This is a topic one can study for a lifetime.

Journaling

As I've noted elsewhere in this book, it's important for coaches to keep an ongoing journal of the information gathered during coaching sessions. I'd like to share a few more thoughts on this kind of journaling as an opportunity for continuous learning.

This journal must be focused on retaining knowledge gained about the salespeople as well as the knowledge coaches learn about themselves and the coaching strategies employed. The entries about the salespeople should primarily be focused on behavior and attitude, while entries about the coach should focus on developing a personal style and testing new coaching strategies and tactics. The effective coach can collect an incredible amount of information during each coaching session. It is critical to develop a system for recording and reviewing this information prior to the following session; otherwise, the sessions bog down and retrace past issues. A journal is a collection device for the coaching awareness gained during earlier sessions as well as insight and knowledge about salespeople and their performance in specific selling situations. The journal doesn't have to be long and detailed. It just has to cover the most important pieces of data—the information most critical to the salesperson's growth, as well as the coach's.

A 4"x6" journal page is enough to collect critical information. You should expect to use two such pages per coaching session. The first page would be dedicated to the salesperson's issues and "stream of consciousness" remarks. Salespeople typically develop streams of consciousness concerning the sales process while journaling, and the coach must notice and understand these in order to help salespeople grow. A typical stream of consciousness involves thoughts derived from actions over time. On the salesperson's page, I record information like thought process, behaviors, themes, and recurring problems in addition to specific successes, which become a growth chart to help me build momentum during future sessions.

A salesperson may observe, after reading his own journal, that each Monday he has extremely negative feelings about cold calling prior to making the first dial. A result of this thinking may be lack of success when he reviews the previous week's appointments set from previous dialing efforts. A simple change of mindset could have a significant impact on dialing success, but without the journal review, the salesperson would never have known this.

The second page is designed to help coaches grow and gain knowledge used to raise their coaching effectiveness. Salespeople probably never realize how much their coaching sessions develop and influence the coach's style and growth. The second page can be focused on the coach's strategies and tactics as well as any insight the coach has gained during the session.

I've shared this additional information on journaling with you here for a very simple reason: It takes a strong commitment from both the salesperson and the coach to keep a journal. Most people fizzle out after twelve or thirteen days and never learn the true value of the journaling process. You and your salespeople should not fall into that category. I want you to use your own journal as a visual recording of progress and to help the salespeople you work with to recognize the link between journaling and success.

WALKING THE TIGHTROPE

Salespeople are responsible for all the choices they make in their professional lives. It's the coach's job to help salespeople grow while at the same time keeping perspective on who owns the problems being dealt with during the coaching session. This requires a certain balance that can feel elusive at times.

Albert Einstein was quoted as saying, "Man must cease attributing his problems to his environment, and learn again to exercise his will"—his personal responsibility. The same observation applies to the coaching experience. Each salesperson needs to own the issues preventing greater success, and the coach needs to help the salesperson deal with the problems in the spaces where they exist.

All too often, the coach takes ownership of the salesperson's success or failure and becomes a hostage to the salesperson's needs. Manipulative salespeople may use an unaware coach to do their thinking and problem solving for them, absolving them of all responsibility. When in doubt, remind yourself that the primary function of the coach is to develop salespeople, not rescue them.

JASMINE'S STORY

Jasmine's team member Susan was an extremely likeable salesperson. Everyone wanted her to succeed. Her sales career had periods of high performance, with many more lower-performing periods interspersed through the years. As her manager, Jasmine thought highly of Susan and made a commitment to help her succeed. Jasmine invested an incredible amount of time coaching and advising Susan on ways to better her performance. Jasmine had high hopes after each session that Susan would turn the corner and expend the effort necessary for a consistently higher level of success. Jasmine felt sorry for Susan; she felt that Susan wanted to do better. She kept trying to get Susan to "see the light," investing time and effort, taking a personal interest in Susan's success, and working tirelessly to get Susan to change.

Jasmine's vice president asked me to get involved because Jasmine was neglecting the other salespeople on the team in her quest to help Susan succeed. I met with both of them and recognized the problem immediately—Jasmine was more committed to Susan's success than Susan was. My first step was to establish a behavior model to be executed between each coaching session. I recommended to Jasmine that she not schedule the next session until she was advised that Susan had executed the new behavior as planned and had the numbers to prove it. This was the investment Susan had to make in order to receive the benefit of Jasmine's coaching time.

Susan had a habit of making her way to Jasmine's office numerous times a day and asking, "Do you have a minute?" Yet the discussions that followed always took more than a minute. I coached Jasmine on keeping the responsibility for success on Susan's side of the desk. This helped Jasmine become more objective in her coaching sessions. Jasmine began to establish boundaries and stopped interrupting her own day to spend time rescuing Susan.

Jasmine established predetermined coaching times and no longer fell prey to Susan's "Do you have a minute?" strategy. By utilizing my coaching recommendations, Jasmine helped Susan stand on her own two feet and take personal responsibility for raising her own performance, instead of manipulating Jasmine to make things right. Jasmine had learned to walk the tightrope an effective coach must walk. She hadn't given up on Susan and wasn't being co-opted by her, either. It's all a matter of balance.

By the way: Susan's performance did eventually improve under the new system, and Jasmine was able to devote more quality time to other members of the team.

BALANCE IS CRITICAL

Here are a few ways to develop balance in coaching sessions.

- **Coaches must build strength and conditioning in salespeople, rather than exercising their own strength on a salesperson's behalf.** This helps salespeople reach their potential and achieve their professional sales goals. Strength is developed by helping salespeople continuously challenge themselves to raise their performance. Conditioning is a result of repetitive reinforcement of new behavior.

- **Salespeople must own their success to avoid "coaching transference."** Coaching transference occurs when the coach takes personal responsibility for the salesperson's goals and works harder than the salesperson to achieve them. When salespeople own their own success, they display unconditional commitment to improvement in all areas of selling, even at the risk of discomfort.

- **There must be clear boundaries between the salesperson and coach.** Salespeople must understand their behavioral responsibilities and the coach's expectations, and not expect the coach to accept excuses for a lack of effort.

- **Salespeople must focus on their own performance regardless of the performance of others.** The coach is responsible for helping to eliminate comparison performance plateaus such as, "I'm not doing badly compared to

Steve!" Performance is not relative. It has to be focused on the standards the salesperson sets individually.

- **The coach must block the emotion of empathy and remain intellectual during the coaching sessions in order to retain objectivity.** If the coach's emotions enter the process, the coach may lose objectivity and become a hostage to the salesperson's situation.

Becoming a high-performance coach takes discipline and commitment. Successful coaches follow a roadmap dotted with success markers to stay on track. They avoid relying on personality and intuition to succeed and continuously gain knowledge on ways to improve the coaching process after each session.

SANDLER COACHING RULES

- Understand the rationale behind the choices a salesperson makes in the course of a sales call.
- Use knowledge about each salesperson to customize the coaching sessions.
- Work to discern and understand the salesperson's stream of consciousness concerning the sales process.
- Guard against moving the salesperson's issues to the coach's side of the success equation.
- Continuously upgrade the methodology used so your coaching doesn't become stale.

CHAPTER ELEVEN

Moving Forward

OVERVIEW

- Sandler coaching philosophy
- Coaching and Sandler's sales and leadership programs
- Best practices
- The Sandler Change Triangle
- Final thoughts

This chapter covers the Sandler coaching philosophy and shows how it is integrated into Sandler's management program. Coaching salespeople must have a cadence that focuses on regular sessions that reinforce one another and become part of the manager's behavior plan.

THE SANDLER COACHING PHILOSOPHY

The focal point of coaching is not determining whether the salesperson is right or wrong in the thoughts or actions of each day. It is finding the most personalized approach to solving problems and releasing issues preventing this particular salesperson from growing in the future.

Recall the Sandler Success Triangle discussed in Chapter Three. Successful coaching involves empowering salespeople to achieve greater success by focusing on their own behavior, attitude, and technique in the context of the sales function. The triangle formed by these three points is the basis for success and the focal point for growth.

DAVID'S STORY

David was still in the early phase of his career. His manager Catalina wanted him to learn all he could about selling, so she sent him to a basic sales training program hosted by the local Chamber of Commerce. The course taught David some traditional ways to build relationships, qualify opportunity, make feature/benefit presentations, and attempt to close for the order.

David absorbed the information like a sponge, learning all he could from the one-day session. During the next two weeks, he put to use all he had learned, and his business showed some improvement. At the 3-week mark, though, David's sales numbers slumped dramatically—and stayed slumped. Catalina asked me to analyze David's problem, determine the issues preventing him from attaining greater success, and make some recommendations on ways to improve his performance. After using assessment tools to evaluate his inner strengths and weaknesses, I concluded that David had the capacity for growth and the behavioral traits to be a top performer.

I enrolled David in weekly sales workshops to learn the Sandler Selling System methodology. He was an eager student. For the first two months David set up regular weekly coaching sessions with me, hoping to eliminate some roadblocks he was experiencing with the methodology but wasn't comfortable discussing in class. The combination of skill-set training supported by coaching energized his growth and built a success track. We proceeded to build a behavior model incorporating the top ten behaviors necessary to drive his success.

By the end of his third month of training, David had gained enough momentum to fuel consistently positive sales results. He and I agreed—as did Catalina—that he should continue the training and coaching routine we had set up. After one year of Sandler training and coaching, he proudly announced he was performing in the top five of his 100-person sales force.

Coaching helped David develop the conviction and commitment for success and gave him an arena to work on issues that directly affected his success. It gave him the support he needed to break free of old, ineffective patterns his training with the other company would have never reached.

How different his story would have been if, instead of reaching out to me for coaching, Catalina had sent him to another one-day seminar.

SANDLER COACHING INSIGHT

The Sandler Coaching Philosophy

- To help salespeople grow and achieve their maximum potential by developing a relationship of trust in which salespeople continuously analyze personal behavior, attitude, and technique.
- To build an environment that encourages salespeople to learn to better execute their skills, strive for improvement, and learn all they can about their profession as well as themselves.
- To understand that sales is a profession where excellence can be achieved and mediocrity is not acceptable.
- To always provide a learning environment where salespeople can challenge their thinking and develop their skills.

The Sandler coaching philosophy stems from two core beliefs: Fundamental success comes from wisdom gained via self-discovery and personal improvement, and salespeople have the potential to be experts within their professional lives. Coaching is more than simply following a methodology to influence a salesperson's life. It is a profound interaction that changes both coach and sales-person. The motivation of the effective coach is the sincere desire to help the salesperson succeed.

Coaches must focus on the big picture and define coaching objectives for each salesperson and session. They must establish guiding principles and nurture every relationship while creating a low-stress environment. Every coaching session should be delivered using the Sandler Coaching System methodology and reflecting the values and principles set down in this book.

COACHING AND SANDLER'S SALES AND LEADERSHIP PROGRAMS

There is a powerful link between the Sandler Coaching System and the sales and management programs taught weekly in Sandler Training centers and on site with corporate clients. The coaching, sales, and management programs all follow the methodical approach David Sandler used to revolutionize selling in 1967 and share consistent strategies and tactics.

David Sandler developed a methodology that champions honest, no-nonsense sales strategies and techniques to elevate selling to the professional level. His systematic approach utilizes a behavior model that, when followed, reliably delivers the desired result from the sales call. Developing relationships with prospects, finding reasons for them to act, and presenting a solution (personalized to prospects' needs) are the keys to Sandler selling success. The same three elements apply to coaching.

The effective coach builds a trust-based relationship with the salesperson, utilizing similar strategies as in the buyer-seller world. Next, the coach finds the hidden reason the salesperson needs coaching; this mutual discovery encourages the commitment necessary to help the salesperson grow. This step is highly personalized and is similar to the process of finding pain in a prospect. It requires both parties to be comfortable with the discomfort surrounding this key discovery. Lastly, the coach helps the salesperson create and implement a customized solution to the problems uncovered.

? WHAT DOES IT MEAN?

Socratic questioning is defined by the Free Dictionary as "(a) pedagogical technique in which a teacher does not give information directly but instead asks a series of questions, with the result that the student comes either to the desired knowledge by answering the questions or to a deeper awareness of the limits of knowledge." The method is historically associated with the Greek philosopher Socrates.

The sales, management, and coaching methodologies described in this book rely heavily on the questioning strategies David Sandler first developed to be used with the Sandler Selling System. He believed that gathering information with effective questions was a powerful way of controlling the outcome of the sales call—as opposed to the tactic of giving information directly (utilized by most ineffective salespeople). Questioning strategies keep the focus on the buyer in the selling process and on the salesperson in the coaching process.

All of this is delivered, using the Socratic method of questioning, allowing both parties to build an atmosphere of exploration and discovery. Here too, the Sandler Coaching System mirrors the Sandler Selling System.

Coaching plays a prominent role in the Sandler management program taught monthly in local Sandler Training centers.

TEN COACHING BEST PRACTICES

You've gotten a lot of information in this book. Often, when I've shared as much as I've shared with you, the people I work with ask me to distill everything I've discussed into a manageable list of best practices—something that can be pinned up on a wall and consulted easily in the course of the working day. With that request in mind, I offer my list of ten coaching best practices you can incorporate to raise your coaching performance.

1. **View coaching as a process, not an event.** This allows growth to be measured over time. Establish a coaching cadence where coaching sessions take place every two weeks at a minimum. Remember, coaching is a salesperson-focused competency designed to help salespeople constantly grow and develop their skills. Build a climate of continuous change in order to prevent plateaus from occurring in the coaching cycle.

2. **Integrate coaching into the company culture.** View it as a key component of the leadership function. Build a

safe, positive, supportive environment in which coaching focuses on achieving goals as well as problem solving.

3. **Instill personal accountability in the mind of the salesperson.** This becomes the fuel necessary for performance improvement. Coaching works best with salespeople who hold themselves to a higher standard of performance and accept that growth is their own responsibility.

4. **Eliminate the "called to the principal's office" mentality.** Coaching is only successful if it is a part of a salesperson's development program, and not viewed as punitive. It is important to eliminate any "gotcha" mentality and to build a positive environment where salespeople associate coaching with personal goal achievement.

5. **Begin with a full assessment of each salesperson.** Understand the salesperson's current level of competency as well as the relevant behavioral drivers.

6. **Resist the urge to simply fix short-term problems.** Fully understand the depth of the issue prior to helping the salesperson deal with it.

7. **Block the urge to get creative or to wing it.** Prepare properly for each session and not get pulled into the "coach on the fly" mentality. Coaching success is directly related to the coach's ability to follow the seven-step Sandler Coaching System to the letter.

8. **Be ready to deal with internal, personal issues the salesperson faces as well as external, more obvious problems.**

Focus on the Sandler concept of self-worth, which incorporates building a strong Identity to support the development of the sales Role. Without this holistic approach, coaching cannot deliver sustainable results.

9. **Build a self-coaching model that the salesperson can use between sessions.** Support the actions taken during the coaching session with reinforcing "homework." This prevents the peaks-and-valleys pattern that can turn coaching into a mercurial rollercoaster ride.

10. **Stick to facts.** Focus on the facts gathered from the salesperson's behavior and recounting of events. There is no place in effective coaching for mind reading. Use questions to probe below the salesperson's version of reality to uncover issues that lie beneath the surface.

Incorporating these best practices will help you create an environment where you and the salesperson can work together to achieve success.

THE SANDLER CHANGE TRIANGLE

Coaching for performance improvement was once associated only with athletic success. Then the business sector began to understand that coaching is a support mechanism for any performance-driven endeavor. Unfortunately, coaching is a field that does not require a certification to enter so there are many unqualified coaches using outdated motivational tactics as a way to raise performance. These "baseball cap and whistle" motivators have the ability to do more harm than good. Their "rah rah" methodology creates short-term growth blips (sometimes) and long-term disappointment (always).

The seven-step Sandler Coaching System I've shared with you in this book is a proven system that, when utilized consistently, will effectively help salespeople make the short- and long-term changes necessary for sustained growth. It develops a formal relationship between the salesperson and coach designed to close the success gap—that is, the space between where the salesperson is currently performing and the desired, elevated level of performance.

The methodology you've learned in these pages creates a blueprint for success known as the Sandler Change Triangle. This model is based on raising salespeople's **capacity** for higher performance, improving **competency** so they can rise above the sales problems holding growth hostage, and expanding **capability** when they are in the selling arena. These three points are used by the effective coach as a guide for developing each salesperson's true potential. Let's look at each point of the triangle in depth.

- **Capacity** is the starting point for success. The salesperson's current expectations for success must be benchmarked and used as the baseline for change. Capacity is simply the maximum amount a salesperson can grow over a given timeframe. Understanding this range eliminates "coaching overload." This happens when a salesperson receives coaching at intervals that don't allow him to execute the behavioral modifications necessary for sustained growth. Once the right capacity expectations are set, they must be calibrated and placed on a coaching timeline for action. Then a new behavior target must be established by both coach and salesperson so progress can be tracked and measured.

- **Capability** is the next point on the triangle. The coach must understand the degree of growth a salesperson is capable of achieving. This involves analyzing the salesperson's attitudes regarding change, his personal history when it comes to making changes, and his dedication to the growth he has set as a goal.

- **Competency** involves an assessment of the salesperson's skill set, knowledge of the Sandler selling methodology, and aptitude or natural level of talent. As I've mentioned, it is extremely important for the coach to understand the salesperson's current level of competency and provide additional Sandler training in another setting if the competency is below the expected standard. (Remember that training is not part of the coaching process.)

Capacity

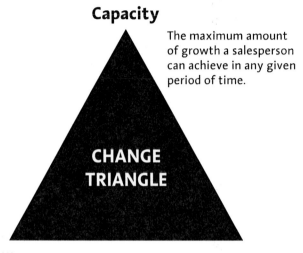

The maximum amount of growth a salesperson can achieve in any given period of time.

CHANGE TRIANGLE

Capability

The degree of growth a salesperson is capable of achieving in the long term. This involves analyzing the salesperson's attitudes regarding change, his personal history, and other factors.

Competency

The salesperson's skill set, knowledge of the Sandler selling methodology, and aptitude or natural level of talent. Requires assessment.

CONNOR'S STORY

Connor is a career salesperson who has received numerous company awards for superior performance. During his most recent performance review, Connor discussed his plan to "get to the next level of growth" with his manager over the next three years. By his own admission, Conner had plateaued. He was afraid his performance would begin to slip without new challenges.

I met with Connor and his manager Jesse to analyze the situation. I used the Change Triangle as a guide for the discussion. Our first discussion centered on defining Connor's expectations for greater achievement. Once those were established, we developed a realistic timeline for achievement. Then we developed a new performance target to stretch Connor's daily behavior routine. Once the capacity point on the triangle was set, we shifted our attention to the capability point of change. We reviewed Connor's attitude about the difficult transition he was about to make and found he had some trepidation that needed to be dealt with as part of the coaching process. This was the first major change in his career. He didn't have the historical experience to know how he would act during such a big transition. He was, however, unconditionally committed to making these improvements, and he felt the challenge would motivate him to higher performance.

A competency review completed the triangle. I found Connor certainly had the skill set, but he needed to work with his Sandler trainer to raise his execution of the Sandler Selling System to a higher level. His talent level was silver on the Olympic medal scale; he needed to improve to gold for greater success.

By using the Sandler Change Triangle, we were able to pinpoint specific areas of improvement necessary to accomplish Connor's goal. With regular coaching sessions, he challenged himself and re-energized his career. His plateau turned into an upward incline.

The Sandler Change Triangle is a powerful tool you can and should use to assess the salesperson's real-world ability to change. In reality, most salespeople are change-averse (though they seldom volunteer this information). They tend to follow familiar patterns and remain in their comfort zones. The Change Triangle helps salespeople understand that change doesn't have to be painful and can be seen as a necessary part of their professional growth.

FINAL THOUGHTS

In order for salespeople to achieve their true potential, they need a skilled coach to guide their growth. The coach's job is to help them through the blind spots in their performance so they can break free from the beliefs and behavior patterns that are holding higher performance hostage. The salesperson, coach, and company each win from effective coaching. They all benefit from the fruits of higher performance.

Successful coaching takes time and preparation to be effective. It challenges the coach to be a facilitator of growth by helping the salesperson challenge his behavior, assumptions, expectations, and awareness, and ultimately by helping redefine winning in a way that supports personal growth on all levels. The methodology I have shared with you in this book fosters self-discovery, which is, in my experience, the most powerful tool for change.

The most effective coaching helps the salesperson focus on becoming rather than just doing. In the end, coaching is as much about becoming a better person as it is about doing better in the sales profession. High-performing salespeople have always understood the impact of Sandler's Identity/Role Theory which has been discussed at length in countless books (including this one) but may be summed up concisely as follows: *Working on who you are is as important as working on what you do.* This holistic approach is the key to success in both training and coaching—and indeed to success in life.

It surprises many sales professionals to learn that the manager, too, needs a coach to help develop and expand coaching skills. Not all managers, though, have committed themselves to a face-to-face coaching relationship. That's where this book comes into play. I designed it to be the starting point of the manager's coaching. It provides a roadmap to improve coaching performance. You can continue the journey by contacting your local Sandler Training center.

Used properly, in conjunction with Sandler coaching workshops, this book can be utilized as a step-by-step process to help all sales professionals achieve higher performance and greater success. You can learn the essentials of the Sandler Coaching System from this book. However, in order to be effective with it, you have to practice it, live it, and reinforce it over time. We're here to help with that. I leave you with a simple challenge: Visit us at www.sandler.com/resources/sandler-books/coaching.

SANDLER COACHING RULES

- Customize the coaching model for each salesperson and personalize each solution.
- Develop an individual leadership style that encompasses the right proportion of supervision, coaching, mentoring, and training.

- Embed sales coaching in the company sales culture as a key driver of success.
- Use the Sandler Change Triangle as a blueprint to help the salesperson achieve maximum potential.
- Allow enough time and thoroughly prepare for each coaching session.

23 Action Steps to Build Coaching Effectiveness

1. Don't wait until you have perfected your coaching process. Begin immediately and realize that effectiveness will improve over time.

2. Help salespeople set long-term and short-term goals that they are 100% committed to achieving. Use the Rule of Three and Two to develop both personal and professional goals. These impact both the Identity and Role. The Rule of Three and Two focuses the salesperson on three professional goals and two personal goals each day. The three

professional goals help the salesperson become more effective in the job, and the two personal goals help the salesperson grow self-worth during the struggles of each day.

3. Begin coaching the middle 60% of your sales force. That's where the greatest impact can be achieved.

4. Coach to the salesperson's current level of skill, knowledge, and application—not where you think the salesperson should be.

5. Incorporate coaching time in your weekly calendar.

6. Set role-plays and practice runs with peers and trusted salespeople in order to help the salesperson experience tactics and strategies in real selling situations, played out in a safe environment.

7. Make sure the salesperson has provided enough background information on the most important issues prior to beginning the coaching process. Information propels success.

8. Determine whether the salesperson is in denial, resistance, exploration, or commitment during the coaching session. The salesperson's position determines the coach's approach to the problem.

9. View the coaching session as a movie. Help the salesperson view the movie in a slow-motion, frame-by-frame process. Don't miss a frame! Missing key details limits the effectiveness of the session.

10. Review the top nine coaching characteristics and attributes

from Chapter Two and rate yourself on a scale of 1 to 10 on each element. Any attribute that cannot be rated at least a 7 must be turned into a goal for improvement.

11. Build a coaching roadmap with behavioral modification mile markers on it to determine progress. A typical mile marker is gradual improvement in setting stronger up-front contracts to better control the sales call.

12. Build an individual Success Triangle for each salesperson, one that is focused on behavior, attitude, and technique. Identify one of the points on the triangle as the focal point for the session. The salesperson can set behavior goals to focus on activity that drives success, attitude goals to strengthen the beliefs that support success, and technique goals to improve skills.

13. Make sure all salespeople are working on and expanding their top ten behaviors necessary for success.

14. Focus coaching on skills, knowledge, and application.

15. Help salespeople plan for success with strategic coaching; help them better execute their existing skills with tactical coaching.

16. Follow the Sandler coaching methodology just as you would the Sandler sales process. Don't "wing it."

17. Develop strategic thinking; utilize the coaching feedback loop to help the salesperson grow.

18. Use journaling to track each salesperson's growth and progress.

19. Keep a personal coaching journal and review it every 90 days to determine negative patterns to be corrected.

20. Help salespeople develop mental toughness by supporting them as they learn how to fail.

21. Build and support a continuous learning environment.

22. Establish minimum behavior expectations and use coaching to raise salespeople's performance.

23. Every coach needs a coach—so contact your Sandler trainer or visit us at www.sandler.com/training-centers.

Look for these other books
on shop.sandler.com:

Prospect the Sandler Way

Transforming Leaders the Sandler Way

Selling Professional Services the Sandler Way

Accountability the Sandler Way

Selling Technology the Sandler Way

LinkedIn the Sandler Way

Bootstrap Selling the Sandler Way

Customer Service the Sandler Way

Selling to Homeowners the Sandler Way

Succeed the Sandler Way

CONGRATULATIONS!

The Sales Coach's Playbook
includes a complimentary seminar!

Take this opportunity to personally experience the non-traditional sales training and reinforcement coaching that has been recognized internationally for decades.

Companies in the Fortune 1000 as well as thousands of small- to medium-sized businesses choose Sandler for sales, leadership, management, and a wealth of other skill-building programs. Now, it's your turn, and it's free!

You'll learn the latest practical, tactical, feet-in-the-street sales methods directly from your neighborhood Sandler trainers! They're knowledgeable, friendly and informed about your local selling environment.

Here's how you redeem YOUR FREE SEMINAR invitation.

1. Go to www.Sandler.com and click on Find Training Location (top blue bar).
2. Select your location.
3. Review the list of all the Sandler trainers in your area.
4. Call your local Sandler trainer, mention *The Sales Coach's Playbook* and reserve your place at the next seminar!